Richard III
The Final 24 Hours

Marcella Mayfair

Then to K*ing* Richard there came a Knight,
& said, "I hold itt time ffor to fflee;
ffor yonder stanleys dints they be soe wight,
against them no man may dree.
"Heere is thy horsse att thy hand readye;
another day thou may thy worshipp win,
& ffor to raigne w*i*th royaltye,
to weare the crowne, and be our K*ing*."
he said, "giue me my battell axe to my hand,
sett the crowne of England on my head soe hye!
ffor by him *tha*t shope both sea and Land,
K*ing* of England this day I will dye!

From the Ballad of Bosworth Field

Then they blew up the bewgles of brass,
That made many a wife to cry, alas !
And many a wives child father lesse ;
They shott of guns then very fast,
Over their heads they cou'd them throw ;
Arrow's flew them between,
As thick as any hayle or snowe,
As then that time might plaine be seene.
Then Rees Ap Thomas with the black raven
Shortly he brake their array ;
Then with thirty thousand fighting men
The Lord Pearcy went his way ;
The Duke of Northfolke wou'd have fledd with a good wi
ll
With twentye thousand of his company,
They went up to a wind millne upon a hill
That stood soe fayre and wonderousse hye,
There he met Sir John Savage, a royall knight,
And with him a worthy company.
To the death was he then dight,
And his son prisoner taken was he ;
Then the Lord Alroes began for to flee,
And so did many other moe.
When King Richard that sight did see,
In his heart he was never soe woe ;
I pray you, my merry men, be not away,
For upon this field will I like a man dye,
For I had rather dye this day,
Then with the Standley prisoner for to be.
A knight to King Richard can say there,
Good Sir William of Harrington,
He said, Sir King, it hath no peere
Upon this feild to death to be done,
For there may no man these dints abide ;
Low, your horse is ready at your hand ;

Sett the crown upon my head that tyde,
Give me my battle ax in my hand ;
I make a vow to mild Mary that is so bright,
I will dye the King of merry England.
Besides his head they hewed the crown down right,
That after he was not able to stand ;
They dunge him downe as they were woode,
The beat his bassnet to his head,
Untill the braine came out with bloode ;
They never left him till he was dead.
Then carryed they him to Leicester,
And pulled his head under his feet

From The Most Pleasant Song of The Lady Bessie

6:03 AM 21st August 1485
The White Boar Inn, Leicester
27 hours and twelve minutes until the death of Richard III

Richard III of England woke after a decent night's sleep.

He had to admit that he had awoken in far more luxurious accommodations than the White Boar Inn in this lifetime. On the other hand, he reflected that he had awoken in far worse as well. He had certainly awoken in some hovels when on campaign with his elder brother Edward IV, or during those dark and bleak months of exile when the turncoat Warwick helped restore the simple minded Henry VI to the throne. *The Kingmaker* many people had called Warwick. At that point Richard had simply called him a bastard. It was a little harsh, considering that he had been brought up in the man's household and had considered him a second father. He had even married his daughter! But for turning against the House of York he was a bastard. *The Kingmaker* wouldn't be interfering in the current games that were going on for the throne: he'd been dead for well over a decade, killed at the battle of Barnet while trying to flee like a coward.

The man who now held the kingmaker's title, Earl of Warwick, was his grandson and Richard's own nephew. He was a simple witted boy and also wouldn't be partaking in this round of games. As the son of the Duke of Clarence, Richard's brother who had suffered from attainder, the new Earl of Warwick had no rights to the throne. Yet, Richard was fully aware that attainders could be reversed in Parliament. Despite his lack of wits, his nephew's title and heritage made him a risk. Some ambitious fool could attempt to rule through him. This was why young Warwick was up at Sheriff Hutton in Richard's heartland of Yorkshire. There he was firmly out of the way and under the watchful gaze of some of the king's most trusted men. As a king without a living son, Richard had to make sure that all potential claimants to his crown were kept close to the throne. Whilst he was dealing with this insignificant and troublesome Welshman, it was quite possible others were plotting new schemes in dark rooms elsewhere.

Richard had plans for the other principle claimant: his brother's daughter, Elizabeth. She too was safely out of harm's way at Sheriff Hutton castle. Richard was all too aware of the Welshman's public declaration the previous Christmas in Reims that he would marry Elizabeth of York and take the crown for himself. He was also fully aware of the plotting that had been going on between the two elderly witches of the royal court, his brother's widow, Elizabeth Woodville, and the vile, scheming, single minded Margret Beaufort. They were the powerhouses behind the Welshman's ambitions. If their two children married and took the throne, then they would see the final unification of the Houses of York and Lancaster. Woodville would like nothing better than to see Richard fall. Even Richard couldn't blame her.

Once the Welshman was defeated, which would only be in a matter of days, then Richard himself would marry his niece – after the formalities of a dispensation from the Pope had been granted of course. Only recently he had been forced to deny that he was planning on marrying Elizabeth of York. But now that his own queen, Anne, was dead, there was nothing in his path to stop him.

There was also the possibility of a foreign princess, but portraits lie. Richard had seen Elizabeth; he knew of her beauty and he was smitten. Advantageously, she would be removed as a player for his throne.

The great game had been played in England for nigh on thirty years. Thousands upon thousands of men had lost their lives in the continual quest for power and glory. Now there were so few claimants to the throne left alive that the ludicrous House of Lancaster had been forced to serve up Margret Beaufort's Welsh son Henry Tudor as their saviour. Someone had to physically sit down with Richard and show him on a family tree how Henry Tudor had a claim to the throne. Richard had laughed when the connections to the crown were pointed out: an illegitimate female line to Edward III. No one in England would accept this man as their king, he had thought. Yet, on this point Richard was mistaken, as clearly some Englishmen did accept it: even now, Henry Tudor rode at the head of a large army not many miles from where he sat.

But Richard was confident. He had every right to be. Richard was a battle hardened military general. The Duke of Norfolk was by his side, as were the Earls of Northumberland, Kent, Shrewsbury, Lincoln, and West Murland.

The Welshman had never fought in a battle. He had spent his life hiding in exile. His only significant noble support came in the form of the Earl of Oxford and of course, his wizened uncle, Jasper. And yet Richard's spies had brought news of defections as Tudor had made his way from Pembroke, Rhys Ap Thomas and Thomas Mitton among them. Milton had vowed that Tudor would only enter England over his body – so much for that vow. Tudor's forces were growing, and Richard had to engage and put an end to this sooner rather than later.

Despite the growing forces of his rival, Richard knew he would win. The odds were still massively stacked in his favour. He was experienced in warfare. He had the nobles. He would march out of Leicester by nine in the morning and choose the ground on which they would fight. He was the one wearing the crown. He was king. He couldn't lose to an insignificant Welshman with a fool's claim on the English throne.

But in amongst his confidence Richard sensed something else.

Doubt.

That doubt focused on one thing:

What was Lord Thomas Stanley planning to do?

6:15 AM 21st August 1485
The Cistercian Abby at Merevale, near Atherstone
27 hours until the death of Richard III

Thomas, Lord Stanley reflected on the clandestine meeting that had ended a little more than half an hour ago.

There were fewer better places that helped with the matter of reflection than the calmness of a Cistercian Abby. Thomas was far less accustomed than his current wife at spending hours in religious devotion. Ever since their marriage, Margret Beaufort had spent more hours at pray than any other person he had ever met. There was no love or passion in their marriage. There never had been and never would be. It was a mutually beneficial political union. As one of the last remaining Lancastrian figures, Margret Beaufort had needed a place of safety within the establishment of the House of York. Thomas Stanley had always been a Yorkist king's man, for her he was the perfect choice. The properties, lands, and wealth that Margret Beaufort had brought with her as the Beaufort heiress, and on the back of two previous marriages, had made the continual plotting and scheming that also came with her just about bearable. It wasn't a match made in heaven, but rather one forged on the bloody and brutal political landscape of the royal houses of England.

Whilst Edward IV was on the throne there was no chance that Margret would have managed to twist Thomas' mind with her treasonous schemes of bringing her exiled son home and to the throne she believed was his. But the colossus that was King Edward was dead, a simple fever doing the job that countless battles could not. Richard, Duke of Gloucester had then usurped the throne from the fingers of his own nephews, in an instant betraying the loyalty to his brother that during his reign had been unquestioned. No one had seen the little Princes for almost three years. Margret had it on good authority that the boys were dead, murdered in their beds and buried somewhere within the dark forbidding walls of the Tower. Thomas hadn't asked on which authority she had found out this information. He rather suspected that if he enquired further then he might not like the answer, and worried that it might end at his own door.

Thomas had come out in support of Richard during Buckingham's rebellion, a rebellion that his wife fully supported and helped finance. She managed to escape with her life after Thomas had intervened. It had actually worked out well for him as Margret was placed under house arrest and her wealth and lands were transferred to his name.

But in recent months, Thomas had begun to have doubts about his king. It could not be contested that Richard had usurped the throne from his nephew, despite the web of lies that had been constructed to suggest the children were illegitimate. Margret kept up a constant stream of promises: yes, he held wealth and a certain degree of power, but what he had now was nothing compared to what he would be awarded if he were step-father to the king.

All he had to do to was help put Margret Beaufort's son on the throne.

It was a tantalising prospect.

Until three hours ago Stanley had never met his step-son. It had been impossible of course, as Henry Tudor had spent the vast majority of life in exile overseas.

But here within the thick walls of the Abbey they had met. It was a place to discuss secrets. Dark secrets. Treason perhaps.

Stanley was impressed with Henry Tudor. He was a tall man with an intensity in his eyes. It struck him that he looked more like a king than Richard, whose physical problems meant that he was walking more bent over than he had ever seen him before. As they talked, Tudor appeared thoughtful and intelligent. Never once did he seem arrogant or conceited.

At the end of the meeting he found himself promising his and his brother's forces to Henry's cause.

But, of course, there were the usual Stanley caveats.

The Stanley's would not be publicly declaring their allegiance and they certainly wouldn't be lining up behind Tudor's Welsh Dragon banner. Thomas Stanley liked to play both sides until he was sure how the dice would land. If he had learnt anything it was the importance of backing the winning side.

Stanley's position was also hampered by the fact that Richard held his son and heir, Lord Strange, as a hostage. Richard's letters had become increasingly more threatening in recent days as he demanded that Stanley bring his forces to Leicester to join the rest of the royal army. Stanley's first gambit had been to say that he was stuck in Nottingham with the sweat. Once that had been cured, then his argument was that he couldn't join with Richard's forces because he was holding Whatling Street for the king, thus preventing Henry Tudor from marching from Lichfield down the roman road to London.

Stanley knew that Tudor wasn't easily fooled. Tudor knew that Stanley had promised himself to both men.

But Stanley believed he had given his step-son hope. And if he helped him to victory then the rewards would be immense.

6:57 AM 21st August 1485
Latham House
26 hours and 18 minutes until the death of Richard III

Margret Beaufort was at prayer.

She scratched her shoulder subconsciously. Her coarse hair shirt worn underneath her garments had caused her all manner of personal discomfort over the recent weeks, yet now more than ever was a good time to be close to Christ.

She knew that it couldn't be long until the battle was fought. Any moment now she might receive news.

She had arranged for a string of young messengers from here to wherever her son's army was that day. She sent him letters each day, completely disregarding the terms of her detainment. Her husband wasn't there to prevent her from doing so, not that he would have tried, thought Margret. Her son wasn't as diligent with his replies, but between his and Jasper's communications she had a fair idea of what was occurring. The support of Rhys Ap Thomas was critical to her son's cause and she had given particular thanks when news of this reached her.

Her husband's communications were few and far between. There was little to read in the short messages he sent her. There was nothing in writing that would incriminate him of treason.

Which way would her husband go?

She prayed harder that he would have the wisdom to make the right choice.

7:30 AM 21st August 1485

Henry Tudor's Camp - Just outside Tamworth

25 hours and forty five minutes until the death of Richard III

Rumour was flying around the camp that their leader was missing.

Increasingly elaborate stories were being told. Some said that Henry Tudor, the man who was calling himself king, had fled and even as they spoke was galloping with his uncle Jasper, Earl of Pembroke, back to Wales. Others said that they had made their way to the Trent in the hope of securing a boat to take them to the coast. Others suggested that they were meeting other rebels in the hope of bringing them to his side. One drunk Welshman had even suggested that he had disappeared to fight a personal duel with Richard III to save anyone from being killed. The French had their own theories, which they kept to themselves. As did the Scots.

The Earl of Oxford could do little to stop these rumours, especially as the basis for them all was true.

Henry Tudor and around twenty of his closest advisers and bodyguards were missing.

Tudor had ordered them to move off whilst he had stayed behind in Litchfield. Oxford was fully aware of why Tudor had stayed behind: he was attempting to arrange a meeting with the Stanleys. The Stanley forces had been shadowing their movements for a number of days, seemingly blocking any attempt Tudor may have had of marching to London. Yet he had expected Tudor's return by now. The army would need to move; he didn't want to delay much longer. The scouts had reported that Richard's forces were in and around the town of Leicester. It was highly probable that the forces would engage within hours. Henry Tudor needed to be present.

Before Oxford had ridden off with the army, he had warned Tudor of the duplicity of the Stanleys. They promise much but deliver little, insisted Oxford. He prayed that Tudor could persuade them to join their forces. The fact that Lord Stanley was married to Tudor's mother should have ensured his loyalty. But Oxford knew that wouldn't be enough. Stanley had always been Richard's man. He believed the best Tudor could hope for was the promise that the Stanley's would not engage with the king's forces. But he would certainly not put it past the brothers to have taken Tudor prisoner and even at that moment be flinging him at the merciless feet of Richard.

Then there was a commotion, and Oxford could see men arising from around the fires. His first thought was that Richard's forces were here. His brother Edward had been famed for pulling surprise attacks: could this be one final devastating surprise for the House of York? But the men didn't seem to be panicked, just inquisitive.

Then he saw them, a group of riders. One, whom he immediately identified as Sir William Brandon, held the banner of Henry Tudor aloft.

He was back.

What had he managed to achieve?

The French troops started to cheer as he passed. They were being paid well enough, so why shouldn't they cheer, thought Oxford.

As he rode closer the Welsh started to gather. Rhys Ap Thomas' forces were numerous. More than the French, Scots, and English combined. The Welsh Dragon in the banner fluttering in the sunlight began to rouse them. Tudor offered a slight wave, but his face remained in the serious expression that he had only ever witnessed on the man's face. He was glad he was not playing him at cards, with a face as fixed as his, he would never give his hand away.

The majority of the English forces were gathered closest to Oxford's tent, all under the command of their various masters. Sir Richard Corbett had been a great blessing bringing almost eight hundred well-armed men to the army. It was these men that Tudor began passing through now, clearly making his way towards him.

The massive bulk that was Sir John Cheny appeared at Oxford's side. "Let us hope he brings good news, My Lord," he said quietly. "The scouts report that Northumberland is nearing Leicester with an additional four thousand."

Oxford's heart leapt at the news, but his face did not betray him. The spies had reported that even if Northumberland's troops did not arrive, they would have been outnumbered. Now with four thousand more men at his disposal, Richard looked almost certain of victory.

Unless, that was, Tudor had brought good news from the Stanleys.

7:40 AM 21st August 1485
The White Boar Inn, Leicester
25 hours and thirty five minutes until the death of Richard III

Richard III of England broke his fast with the Duke of Norfolk and the Earls of Surrey, Kent, Shrewsbury and Lincoln.

"Never was there a more appropriate name for an inn to set forth from to battle, your Grace," offered Norfolk between mouthfuls of bread, cheese, and cold chicken.

Richard glanced around the assembled men, all of them with a small white boar pinned to their chests. It was Richard's personal badge. They nodded their approval of Norfolk's statement.

"I wonder if Tudor is awaking at an inn called the Welsh Bastard?" said Kent flippantly.

Everyone erupted into laughter, including Richard.

"My Lords," began Richard after the laughter had died down. "It is true what the good Earl of Kent says. Tudor has no hereditary right to my throne. The line that he springs from is not only the female lineage, but it is illegitimate at that. His grandfather was a mere serving man that forced himself upon a weeping widowed queen. A man that should have had his entrails removed in front of his eyes, if the matter had been handled appropriately. Remember that, my Lords. That is what you must impress upon your men this day. God shines on those that He has raised high. I and I alone am the rightful king of England, the next king of the noble line of York. Our line doesn't spring from Welsh serving men. My father was unable to wear the crown himself, but his sons have worn it for him." As the king paused to gathered his thoughts, Norfolk nodded, remembering Richard, Duke of York, the man after whom the present king was named. The man whom the present one so closely resembled in appearance and deed. He had made a play for the crown, quite rightfully so in Norfolk's opinion, yet unlike his sons he had never worn it. The Lancastrians mocked the great man after they had captured him at Wakefield and when they had sliced off his head, they had placed it upon a pike at Micklegate Bar at York. A paper crown was placed upon it as a sign of his ambition and humiliation. This was something Norfolk knew the king had not forgotten. He had watched him command the vanguard of his brother's forces in battle after battle and he knew that inside Richard had been fighting to avenge his father. He knew that very soon he would be fighting again, this time not to avenge his father or to protect his brother's crown. This time Richard would be fighting for himself.

The king cleared his throat and continued. "When we ride out of this town to defeat this Welsh nobody, I will be riding at the head of this great army. The men will know that I am their rightful king and that they will fight for me like true and noble Englishmen. Tudor brings with him only French peasants, Breton thieves, Scots mercenaries, and Welsh inbreds. The English that have sworn allegiance to him are so few that Shrewsbury here has probably swived more serving wenches."

More laughter filled the room at Richard's jest.

“Aye, your Grace,” replied Shrewsbury. “Although I did have another last night.”

The men laughed again until a man appeared in the doorway and looked over at the king waiting to be given approval to enter. Richard noticed him and waved him over. The room grew silent.

He bent down and whispered in Richard’s ear. At first the king’s face was impassive, then it erupted into an uncontrollable grin.

“Gentleman, make space at the table. It seems that finally the Earl of Northumberland has had the good grace to join us.”

9:00 AM 21st August 1485
The White Boar Inn, Leicester
24 hours and fifteen minutes until the death of Richard III

The Earl of Northumberland sat on his horse next to the Duke of Norfolk, waiting for the king to appear.

His progress from the North had been slower than he had wished as he had spent time gathering as many men as he could to the king's cause. After much effort he had managed to bring some four thousand with him. This had caused great cheer from the king and the other lords after his arrival that morning.

He apologised profusely to His Grace for the delay. The king's letters had become harsher in tone over the previous few days; it was obvious from reading them that Richard had believed that he may not be coming, or worse, that he was taking his troops over to Tudor. Nothing could have been further from the truth and he had pushed his men as hard as he dared, though he was only too aware that at some point after this march they would have to fight. It would be little use to the king to bring him four thousand sick and exhausted men.

After the Earl had joined the rest of the lords that morning, it soon became clear that the reason for Richard's doubts were caused by the game currently being played with Stanleys. Northumberland looked down the impressive line of nobles with their standards flying behind them and saw Lord Strange at the far end. Strange was Lord Thomas Stanley's eldest son. He was dressed in his armour as though heading for battle, just like every other noble present. Despite appearances Strange was little more than a prisoner, held by Richard to ensure that his father remembered which side he must fight on. He was glad that he wasn't in Strange's shoes — he rather thought that Stanley might decide to do what favoured him the most despite the predicament of his son.

Loud cheers erupted and Northumberland turned his head.

Richard had appeared. He was dressed in armour, the royal coat of arms emblazoned on his tabard. Before he mounted his horse, which was also wearing armour and the royal coat of arms, he accepted his helmet from a valet. In case there was any doubt who the man was, the helmet was topped with a brilliant gold circlet crown. With great pomp and showmanship he placed it upon his own head as the cheers reached their crescendo. He mounted and moved along the assembled line of the greatest and most powerful men in the land. Behind him went his banners, the Royal Standard, the White Boar, and the Sun in Splendour of the House of York.

Richard was a true king and he was telling the world so by this display.

Northumberland was glad he had ignored the letters from Tudor.

He had chosen the right side.

9:12 AM 21st August 1485
Leicester
Just over twenty four hours until the death of Richard III

Robert Jackson watched the army stream past and could not help but to feel relief.

His employer, William Garston, emerged smiling from the darkness of his rooms to join him.

It has been a highly profitable three and a half days for William. He was a lawyer. One of the few to serve the town of Leicester. Ever since the army began assembling in the town he had a constant stream of knights, gentlemen, and even common men knocking on his door.

The reason?

They knew they were heading to battle. And they knew that not everyone would be heading home again.

Robert Jackson was William's principle clerk and he had not even made it home for the two previous nights. His hand had cramped at writing out more Last Wills and Testaments than he could ever imagine. It seemed that few of those heading to battle had made provisions for their deaths and all rushed in order to do so at the last opportunity.

William would be counting the profit for weeks. Robert did not begrudge it, for he too would receive reward – William was a fair employer in that regard. But it was not William who had to write up the copies of the documents.

To be fair it had been interesting work. He learnt that one knight had no legitimate children but was eager for his two bastard sons to share his estate if he should perish. He learnt that another was in debt to the king himself and had ordered that his lands be sold to pay back the crown, the remainder to his daughter. He learnt that one country gentlemen had debts that would frighten a duke: his poor wife would receive next to nothing once all the settlements were made. And he learnt that one common man, who had not two shillings to his name, desired the lawyers to send a letter home to his wife telling of his regret that he had not been a better husband. Robert had thought it odd as the wife could doubtless not read, just as her husband could not write. But who was he to question the wishes of a man that believed he would soon die.

As he watched the line of men disappear Robert suddenly felt something else.

Guilt.

In a matter of hours many of these men would be dead. And he would still be here complaining about the cramps in his hand. He decided that he had the far better deal.

9:15 AM 21st August 1485
The Church of St Mary de Castro, Leicester
Twenty four hours until the death of Richard III

Father Edward de Alne prayed alone in his church.

Just like the lawyers less than a stone's throw away, he too had had a terribly busy past three days. He was too old for this he had decided. He must visit the bishop and request that he be allowed to retire in peace. He had been priest in Leicester for just over forty years. It was time to pass the torch over to a younger man.

The majority of those that had constructed their Last Will and Testament with Mister William Garston then felt moved to give a final confession of their sins. In fact, Father de Alne also saw many of those that could not afford the services of the lawyer or indeed had rarely any worldly goods that they needed to bequest. It did not matter the amount of wealth a man had: they all needed spiritual strength at a time such as this.

Just like Robert Jackson he had learnt many secret things over the last few days. He had heard confessions from thieves, adulterers, rapists, and even murderers. Each was blessed and sent on their way.

It wasn't just confession that was busier than normal. Masses were packed to the rafters. Yesterday even the King of England himself was in attendance.

Father de Alne had spoken to Richard following the service and told him the story of how, as a younger priest, he had been in attendance in this very church as the young King Henry VI had knighted Richard's father.

Both men had reflected the irony of it. Richard Plantagenet, Duke of York, was knighted in this very church by the man whom he had risen up against later in life. Now the man's son, Richard III of England, was visiting the same church before riding out to finally end the series of wars that his father had started.

Father de Alne had been stuck by the look in the king's eye as he told the tale. It burned with an intensity that he had never seen before. He had asked if the king would like him to hear his confession. Richard graciously declined stating that he had his own confessors with him. In many ways the priest was relieved — even in Leicester they had heard the rumours that surrounded the king. To find out the truth from the man's own lips might be have been too much for him.

He knew that even at that moment Richard was marching into battle.

The priest prayed to God for his safe keeping.

9:20 AM 21st August 1485

Bow Bridge, Just outside the West Gate of Leicester

Just less than twenty four hours until the death of Richard III

Twelve-year-old John Barton and his eight-year-old brother Paul were standing just yards from the far side of Bow Bridge.

The brothers had been in a constant state of excitement ever since the troops started arriving with the Duke of Norfolk a few days ago. Then the rumour started flying around town that the king himself was lodged in the White Boar Inn. Just imagine the King of England lodging in their town! They could scarcely believe it.

Their excitement reached its fever pitch as they watched the arrival of Sir Robert Brackenbury who had brought with him all manner of cannons from the great Tower of London itself. They saw the shiny artillery with cart after cart of shot and cannon balls and imagined the noise and the devastation that it all would cause.

John had wanted to go with the army and fight for the king, but his mother forbade it. He was too young she said. What did she know? He had worked in the fields since he was five and was as strong as any fifteen-year-old. He had thought of disobeying his mother and then thought better of it. His father had died fighting at Barnet for old King Edward. He had been enlisted by their local lord and marched the length of the country just to die. John hadn't wanted him to go, nor had his mother. But his father had said that it was a matter of great honour to fight for a king. John had come to realize that he had had no choice; the lord would have forced him to go or have him tried and executed as a traitor. John had always believed he would follow in his father's footsteps and be a hero fighting for the king of England. But he knew that his time would come. There had been battles aplenty since he was born, and no doubt there would continue to be battles aplenty in the years to come. At present he needed to help his mother put food on the table. Dreams of war and battle would have to wait.

"Is that the king?" demanded Paul prodding his brother in the ribs as Richard rode across the Bridge.

John Barton had no idea, but the crown on the helmet gave a clear message. "Aye, that is the king."

Richard smiled down at the children as he rode past. That is how a king should look, thought John. He couldn't help himself and he shouted out, "God keep you safe, your Grace."

Richard nodded his acknowledgement and kept on riding.

The boys stood awestruck for the next thirty minutes as line after line of men marched over the narrow bow bridge in the direction of East Shilton.

As they watched them disappear into the distance, John wondered just how many of them would be coming back.

10:04 AM 21st August 1485
Henry Tudor's Army - On the road to Merevale
23 hours and 11 minutes until the death of Richard III

Lewes Ap Griffith was marching as part of Henry Tudor's personal bodyguard.

His father and grandfather before him had served Jasper Tudor when he was the only Earl and was living in Pembroke Castle. Lewes was just a few years older than Henry Tudor, but he remembered the full horrors of the Yorkist victories and the destruction of the House of Lancaster. He saw Jasper Tudor displaced from his rightful position and forced overseas while William Herbert was given his Earldom and the wardship of Henry Tudor. Lewes' father had continued to serve the new Earl, but inside his loyalty lay with Jasper. Often Lewes caught his father wrestling with his decision but these were times to survive, as his mother would whisper in his ear. You did what you had to do. If that meant switching sides and serving a new Earl, then so be it.

Lewes was one of the first to join Henry Tudor after he had landed in Pembroke.

Jasper Tudor had remembered him once he had explained who he was, and had the good grace to ask after his father. Dead, Lewes had to report. Consumption. Two years past. Jasper had passed on his condolences and immediately appointed him as his nephew's bodyguard. Loyal men were needed close at hand, Jasper had confided, there were too many foreigners. What were needed were loyal Welshmen. Very few of these loyal Welshmen had joined Tudor as he proceeded and Lewes could see that this had worried Jasper Tudor. They had tried to explain Henry Tudor's lineage and tried to make much of the prophecies that he was the true Prince that was spoken of. Yet still they didn't join in any great numbers. Gruffydd Rede and his men were one small group that did. Jasper Tudor welcomed them as though they were a thousand heavily armed cavalrymen. A few others, Richard Griffith and Evan Morgan who were officers of the Herberts, also joined Tudor's army. But still it wasn't enough. Rhys Ap Thomas' force was a godsend. His troops looked like they could have annihilated the rest of the army. If Rhys Ap Thomas had kept his oath to the king, then Tudor's conquest could very easily have been over before it had started. Jasper Tudor had his army of loyal Welshmen.

There had been great concern of the rumoured size of the King's force. Men that might just as easily have been boys were speaking of it in hushed voices when camp was stuck each night.

Yet just a matter of hours ago Henry Tudor had returned to camp, declaring in cryptic words that there would be others joining them.

Everyone knew that must mean the Stanleys. With the Stanleys fighting for Lancaster and Tudor there was hope.

Lewes smiled to himself, for some reason he found it very amusing that within a matter of hours a Welshman might become the king of England.

10:30 AM 21st August 1485
The East Shilton Road
22 hours and forty five minutes until the death of Richard III

The army halted, just over one hour into its march.

Richard was meeting with the Duke of Norfolk and The Earl of Northumberland, also present were two scouts who had just ridden up to the column.

"They were camped outside the castle at the town of Tamworth, your Grace. Just short of twenty miles away I would say.," the younger of the two scouts reported. "There seemed to be no urgency about moving onward this sunrise."

Richard remained silent, seemingly taking in the news.

"Their numbers?" demanded the Duke of Norfolk when it was clear that Richard wasn't about to speak.

"I would say about seven thousand. When in camp it is harder to judge than when they are marching." The scout responds. Norfolk nodded as though that were obvious. "We have left two men to report on their direction when they move."

"Well done boy," stated Richard warmly. "You have served me well."

"Thank you, your Grace," replied the young scout with a slight bow, "There is something else though."

“Tell me,” said Richard, his tone changing.

The younger scout looked over towards the older one. It was clear that this was his part of the story to tell.

“Your Grace. It seems that the forces of my Lord Stanley are currently near the town of Atherstone. It is not clear which direction they are moving. But I have to report that I witnessed a small force of mounted men, twenty-five strong in number, leaving the nearby Abby one hour from dawn. I followed them.” The scout paused for a moment about to deliver his coup de grâce. “They rode towards Tamworth, around four miles before the town, and they raised their banners. They were the Red Dragon. I immediately turned and came to report.”

Once again silence was the response from the king as he contemplated the latest information. Tudor had been visiting the Abby close to the camp of the Stanleys. He feared he knew the reason.

“Anything else?” asked Northumberland. “No indication as to why they were there?”

“I could not stay” replied the scout. “I came to make my report and met Nathaniel here en route.” He indicated the younger man as he spoke.

Richard nodded, “Gentlemen I thank you well. Please return and send further news as you have it. We will continue on this route.”

August 1485
Sheriff Hutton, Yorkshire
Twenty hours and fifteen minutes until the death of Richard III

Elizabeth of York was dining in the great hall.

Her cousin, the Earl of Warwick was doing the same. He wore a vacant look on his face and Elizabeth knew that he would rather be chasing the chickens around the yard outside. She felt nothing but pity for him. How must it be to be like him? To understand so little of what was going on around him and who he actually was in the world.

Elizabeth had no such problem. She knew perfectly well who she was. She was the Niece of the King of England. The Daughter of the King of England. The Sister of the King of England. She also knew that whatever happens on a muddy battlefield she would be the wife of the King of England. And one day she would be the mother of the King of England. Her younger sister assured her that no woman in history had ever been so closely associated with the throne.

Whichever of the two men emerged victorious on the battle would want her hand in marriage. Whichever of them won it would be very fortunate. Elizabeth was fully aware of the affect she had on men. She captivated them, bewitched them even.

She had certainly bewitched her uncle. The whole court was aware of it. Richard had been accused of poisoning his wife in order to marry her. He had been forced to deny it. But now that the queen was dead there was nothing stopping Richard from taking what he wanted, and she knew he wanted her. Richard had tried to keep his hands off her, but failed miserably. Elizabeth had led him on of course, encouraging him at every opportunity.

Her mother had recently encouraged the practice. She had hoped to rule through her son. But now, her last opportunity of influence and power was if her daughter became queen. Even as she let Richard touch her she couldn't help think about her brothers and their fate. She had never asked. She could guess. But she didn't want Richard to confirm it. The thought of lying next to their murderer was unthinkable. But at the same time she wanted Richard as well. The power he held was seductive.

Of course, her mother had wanted vengeance for her sons, especially after Richard had first claimed the throne as his own. It was then that her mother plotted with the Lady Margret and agreed that she should marry Margret's exiled son Henry. Together the two mothers had plotted that Henry would invade and claim the throne and then marry Elizabeth. Elizabeth could see the sense in it from Margret Beaufort's perspective. Everyone knew that she had always clung to the Lancastrian cause and harboured thoughts that one day her son would be king. Of course the man had such a weak claim to the throne that the only way for him to add any legitimacy to it would be to marry her and thus in a stroke unify the House of Lancaster with the House of York. But of course their grand plan had failed with the Duke of Buckingham's rebellion. The Lady Margret had barely escaped with her head and she rather believed Richard had been lenient with her mother because of his desire for her.

She knew that for Henry Tudor the matter had not ended with Buckingham's failed rebellion. He had marched into Rennes Cathedral and vowed not only to claim the crown but to marry her as well. She knew that his desire to marry her was purely for her links to the throne. She had never met the man, although she was sure that he would not be disappointed if the two ever met. Richard's desire was nothing to do with her links to the throne. She breathed a little heavier just thinking about it.

One thing was certain: whichever man won the day would want her to be his wife. Another thing was certain: whoever won, she was sure to accept.

Yet there was one tantalizing thought in the back of her mind.

What if both men perished?

Who would come forward to claim the throne then?

Who would want to marry her for her links to the crown?

Maybe there would be no-one.

No woman had ever sat on the throne of England in her own right.

If ever there was a woman qualified to do it, it was her.

Then she could marry whomever she chose.

2:15 PM 21st August 1485

The road between Tamworth and Atherstone, Leicestershire

18 hours until the death of Richard III

Henry Tudor's scouts are bringing reports that Richard III had left the town of Leicester at the head of a great army.

They are heading in their direction.

Henry knew that the moment of his destiny was almost upon him. It was something he had borne in private for the majority of his life. Ever since the saintly Henry VI had laid his hands upon him and declared that one day he would be king of England. Very few people had witnessed the event. Even less of those that did took it seriously. However, his mother certainly had. From that moment on her life had been dedicated to one thing. Placing her son on the throne of England.

Although he had little contact with his mother, for his life he rather wished that she could be here at this divine moment. Her blessing would do him more good than even the thickest suit of armour.

He dismisses the scouts and the army proceeds. Tomorrow would be a day of battle, death and with god's will glory.

The thoughts of his mother play on his mind.

He knows that he won't be at peace until he resolves them.

He rides in silence and ponders.

4:30 PM 21st August 1485

Somewhere between Bosworth and Sutton Cheney, Leicestershire

16 hours and forty five minutes until the death of Richard III

The scouts reported to Richard that Tudor's army was heading down the Roman Road from Tamworth towards Atherstone.

Both armies were within a few hours' march of each other.

Tomorrow would be a day of battle.

Richard was glad of it.

On the morrow Tudor would be dead, Lancaster would finally be without an heir, and once again he would be rightfully confirmed as the King of England.

He glanced back at the army that followed him. His army. Assembled out of loyalty to their king.

Before they fought he would remind them of just who he was.

5:45 PM 21st August 1485
Ambion Hill, Leicestershire
15 hours and thirty minutes until the death of Richard III

Richard III surveyed the landscape from the top of a hill. The local scout told him that the people call it Ambion.

Ambion Hill gave him a good line of sight over the local terrain. The hill benefitted from protection provided from the narrow ridge and some wetland below. His experienced eyes picked out these features almost instantly and immediately processed their usefulness to his cause.

He remembered the battle lessons that had served the House of York well over the last twenty years.

Choose the ground.

Have the sun and wind behind you.

Richard asked confirmation of the direction of the town of Atherstone together with the direction of the old roman road from the town. The local scout pointed in a direction approximately south-west. Unless he inexplicably changed course this was surely the way that Tudor would come.

Richard knew that he had the superior force. He knew that he had the benefit of the ordnance from the Tower. This hill would have been ideal for a battle. Higher ground, thus making the enemy march on him uphill into his line of fire. But there was a problem. His force was too large to be crammed into such a small space. With the benefit of numbers, he needed space to make those numbers work to his advantage.

Following the line of the sight towards the roman road, he saw large flat areas. A few small villages interrupted the fields, but there would be space enough.

The king spoke in hushed tones to the scout. There were areas of wet marshland out there, the scout advised, but there was firm ground aplenty and areas of slight elevation that were hard to make out from their current position high on Ambion Hill.

The king nodded with satisfaction.

Richard had chosen his ground.

Somewhere between Ambion Hill and the roman road would be where he would make his stand.

"We will camp here tonight," Richard said and immediately men leapt into action. "Tomorrow we will arise early for battle."

7:00 PM 21st August 1485
Ambion Hill, Leicestershire
14 hours and fifteen minutes until the death of Richard III

Richard was praying alone in his tent.

Doubts had filled his mind since he had retired to his tent to rest.

After a long day in the saddle his back was paining him. He completed the stretches that his physicians prescribed, but they brought him little relief.

In front of Norfolk, Northumberland, and the rest, he would show no self-doubt, and certainly no pain. But it was when he was alone that his demons came.

He did not doubt his validity to the throne. That was beyond question: The House of York were the rightful rulers of the realm and he was the true heir of York. Tudor's absurd claim was based on bastardization and was laughable by comparison. Yet he knew from his education that William the First, The Conqueror, was also a bastard. Unlike Tudor, he didn't try to hide it as most called him William the Bastard, some even to his face. Yet he invaded and claimed the throne of England by right of conquest. Tudor had invaded. Was Tudor a new conqueror? Would he claim Richard's throne by right of conquest?

He knew his abilities as a general and a warrior far outweighed his opponent. Tudor had not yet even been in battle.

He had the superior force. His army was built of loyal men. Men that were turning out for their king. Despite the defections he had heard about during the day, Tudor had a handful of Englishmen at best. Tudor's most trusted men were paid mercenaries. If it was one thing he knew it was that paid men wanted to enjoy their money. They would flee when battle turned bloody. Why die for a handful of coins? Then there were the Welsh, who had raised themselves in rebellion in the past and failed miserably. Why would this rebellion be any different?

He had chosen the ground. He would have the sun at his back.

Everything would be to his advantage.

And yet…the doubt was there.

There was still no word from Stanley.

Richard decided if on the morn Stanley did not line up on his side, then Strange would die. A king had to carry out his threats, otherwise they are not threats at all.

Even if Stanley lined up with Tudor, Richard would still have the superior force.

There should be no doubt.

But there was.

And it troubled Richard even more than his accursed back.

7:10 PM 21st August 1485

The Cistercian Abby at Merevale, near Atherstone

14 hours and five minutes until the death of Richard III

The Abbott was ranting at Jasper Tudor, who was ranting back in return.

The army had been camped outside the Abby for less than an hour and already damage had been inflicted to the buildings. The Abbott was none too happy about it and was making his feelings known to Jasper, who had been the one to seek permission for them to camp there.

The Abbot had not particularly desired thousands of hardened soldiers around his Abby and yet he was wise enough not to refuse. One tended to agree with anything that the leaders of an army outside your doors proposed. He knew that many of the crops that were just becoming ready for harvest would be lost, that armies consumed everything in their path – he simply trusted that he would receive fair recompense for them. However, he had assumed that as a house of God everything else would be left as it were. But there was already damage to the beautiful stained glass windows. Minor items were missing. He dreaded what else might occur while the army was camped there.

Inside Jasper Tudor was seething with anger. The Abbott clearly had a point. He had little doubt the fault lay at the feet of the Bretons. Maybe a handful of the French were also not averse to a spot of pillaging when the opportunity arose. Quite simply many of their men were heathens without morals. Yet, his nephew needed them. Heathens tended to fight like dogs but they had no desire to see their maker. Tomorrow Henry Tudor would need as many men as he could muster to fight like dogs for him.

Because of that Jasper Tudor was forced to argue back with Abbott.

The Abbott finally dropped his protests when Jasper assured him that when his nephew was King, full recompense would be given.

The Abbott disappeared to move the gold plate. Just in case. Assurances were one thing, but they would come to nothing if by the end of the morrow Henry and Jasper Tudor were lying dead in the dirt.

8:00 PM 21st August 1485
Latham House
13 hours and fifteen minutes until the death of Richard III

A messenger had arrived.

Margret Beaufort was interrupted from her evening prayers to receive it.

She prayed that it was the news that she was hoping for.

It was a message from her son. But it told her little.

It was written the previous evening and said that he was camped at Tamworth Castle and that a meeting had been arranged with her husband at dawn the next day. He also told her that he had received numbers of men defecting from Richard's army.

Tamworth was not far from Leicester where she knew Richard was camped. The two armies would soon meet. In fact, for all she knew they may already have done so. She hoped that her husband had finally agreed to pledge his support for her son: he knew that the success of his endeavour may well depend upon it.

She decided that this was not to be a night for sleep. Tonight she would conduct a vigil.

She would pray for the wisdom of her husband and the safety of her son.

9:15 PM 21st August 1485
The Cistercian Abby at Merevale, near Atherstone
Twelve hours until the death of Richard III

Henry Tudor sat around the fire with his Uncle Jasper. They are alone for Henry needed to ask something of his uncle.

Henry began by thanking the man he considered a father for everything that he had done for him.

Jasper laughed it off in his normal jovial style.

But Henry was serious. He told his uncle that he has something very important for him to do.

"Of course, my boy, tell me and it is done. As long as it doesn't involve speaking to that Abbott again," he laughed.

Henry managed a short smile and took a deep breath, "I don't want you to ride to battle with me on the morrow."

Jasper was stunned. "How have I offended you?"

Henry raised his hand to hush the objections, "Don't be ridiculous, Uncle. I don't want you to ride to battle at all." Jasper looked very confused. Surely at this defining moment Henry would want him at his side. No. Surely Henry would need him at his side.

"Listen, Uncle," started Henry once more. "We are not saying it, but we both are aware that tomorrow could easily turn ill. And what then would become of my Lady

Mother?" Jasper listened intently. "I would like you to stay here on the morrow as we ride off. I will leave a string of messengers to bring you news. If we fail and I am killed, then I will trust you to go to my Lady Mother and take her to safety. France or wherever. But out of England."

Jasper tried to object, "Henry, when you go into battle I want to be there at your side."

"I know, Uncle, and I would want you at my side. Yet I would be more restful of mind to know that you are ready to ensure the safety of my Lady Mother. If we are victorious then you escort her down to London. I know that she would rather no other."

Jasper Tudor could see that his nephew's mind was made up. Reluctantly, he agreed.

10:15 PM 21st August 1485
Ambion Hill, Leicestershire
11 hours until the death of Richard III

Richard was walking around his camp. He was surrounded by loyal men and he had no fear.

He watched men eating roasted rabbit which they had snared. He watched them drinking ale and singing songs. Not for the first time in his life he half wished that he were one of them. The burdens of kingship were at times too great. At times he would give anything to be without a care, living on the food he could catch or grow and chasing the pretty girls from the local town.

But he knew that was not what God had called him to.

He had been called to greatness.

He was a king.

And he knew that tomorrow evening he would still be a king.

He left his men to their songs and headed back to his tent to sleep.

4:52 AM 22nd August 1485
The King's Tent, Ambion Hill, Leicestershire
4 hours and 23 minutes until the death of Richard III

Richard awoke with a jolt and sat upright in bed. His heart was racing and sweat poured off his body as though he had a raging fever.

Richard knew that it wasn't a fever. Just a nightmare.

It was vivid. So real. They were coming for him. The demons coming for his crown. The clutching hands of children, boys, grasping for the gold circlet around his head. He was fighting them off, but still them came.

He shook his head, attempting to clear his mind of the visions that had seemed so real.

The cool light of dawn helped banish the demons to the nighttime world in which they belonged.

He rose slowly, feeling his heart start to slow to its normal steady rhythm in his chest.

He yawned. Sleep had been hard to come by that night and when it came it was filled with demons. Others might have considered it an omen. His brother Edward certainly would have done. He was far too much influenced by the witch Woodville he had married. Richard considered it no such thing. He took it for what it was. It was simply a nightmare, nothing more, nothing less.

As the sweat dried on his naked body he raised his arms in the air and began the stretches for his back.

It was a nightmare, he told himself again.

Nothing else.

It wasn't an omen.

Already the memory was being to fade.

5:20 AM 22nd August 1485
The King's Tent, Ambion Hill, Leicestershire
3 hours and 55 minutes until the death of Richard III

Richard was having his armour strapped to him. He always savoured the slow and laborious process. A nervous knight would spend the time worrying and wishing it were over so that he could put his mind somewhere else.

However, Richard was not a nervous knight.

He had fought in many battles. He knew what was to come. People always talked about the terrible sights of a battle. For Richard, it was always the noise of the battle that got his heart racing. The sound of steel on steel. The deathly whistle of arrows soaring into the air. The hooves of the horse in the cavalry charge. The groans and screams of the injured and dying. In this battle there would be the explosions of the ordnance to add to that equation. A battle not only looked horrific. It sounded and smelt horrific too.

But Richard knew what to expect. It would be Tudor's first.

Richard rather suspected his enemy was a nervous knight that morning.

As he stood there with the heavy iron plates being strapped to his legs he imagined the way the battle would go. Norfolk would lead the Vanguard. Richard himself the middle. And the rear would be held by Northumberland. He could see Tudor's men advancing and then the image would be obliterated with a blinding flash. The ordnance from the Tower would roar into life. When the light clears he would see Tudor's forces torn to pieces. But they would come again and again and his forces would have to hold. Finally, Tudor's line would break. Norfolk would advance, and Richard would know that this will be a comprehensive victory.

But his men will need to hold firm under Tudor's first attack.

What he planned next was designed to ensure they remembered that they must hold firm.

They had to hold firm because they were fighting for the king.

5:45 AM 22nd August 1485
Ambion Hill, Leicestershire
3 hours and 30 minutes until the death of Richard III

Richard III emerged from his tent at the top of Ambion Hill.

He was dressed in his armour which is polished to a perfect shine. His surcoat proudly displayed the royal standard: the three lions of England and the three fleurs de lis of France, which show the dynastic claims of the English king on the kingdom of France. Four knights clutch silver-clad poles holding the great canopy of estate which is raised above the king's head.

The majority of Richard's men had already gathered in full battle dress at the foot of the hill. His personal bodyguard remained on the crest of the hill. Everyone was watching intently in awed silence.

It was just the way that Richard intended.

Walking in front of the king was a priest holding a large processional crucifix aloft. Four large roundels on each branch of the cross contained the symbol of the House of York: The Sun in Splendour. Behind the priest came the banners, The Royal Standard, The House of York Standard, and Richard's Personal Standard of the White Boar.

Then came the king and the knights holding the canopy of estate.

Behind Richard came the Earl of Northumberland carrying the traditional coronation crown of England; St

Edward's Crown. The jewels that emblazon it danced in the morning sunlight and captured everyone's eye. Northumberland was flanked by the other earls, all of whom had their own standard bearers behind them.

At the rear of the procession came the Duke of Norfolk, Earl Marshal of England holding a small golden bottle. He in turn was flanked by two more priests swinging golden incense carriers.

As the procession passed the lines of Richard's bodyguard they could not help but to gasp at the crown.

The presence of the crown on the battlefield was Richard's masterstroke. When he had issued the order to Brackenbury to assemble with the ordnance from the Tower he had also instructed him to bring the crown. Brackenbury had told no-one of the king's secret order. He personally collected it from where it was under guard with the rest of the crown's jewels in the White Tower. He placed it within a simple, yet very secure chest. He simply instructed two trusted men that they needed to protect the small chest with their lives. The two men wondered what on earth was within the chest, each coming up with more elaborate suggestions as the journey proceeded.

When he reached the crest of the hill the priest stood aside with the cross still held high.

Richard took centre stage.

He knelt on the ground, under the canopy of estate. Norfolk came forward and poured a little of the liquid out of the golden bottle he had been caring. It was holy oil.

He anointed Richard with the sign of the cross on his forehead. Then Norfolk turned to Northumberland and took the crown from his hands and raised it above his head. Richard's hand's received it and Norfolk stood aside. Richard whispered a prayer to himself.

To the army assembled below it looked like a hugely dramatic pause.

Finally, Richard raised the crown and placed it upon his own head. With the crown on his head he rose to his feet. As he stood, Norfolk and Northumberland sank to their knees. Taking their queue from the senior nobles, the rest of the army fell to their knees.

The coronation's reenactment had been solely Richard's idea. He fully understood the symbolism associated with the process. He was renewing his kingship afresh, wiping away the sins of the pasts. Richard was fully aware of the dark rumours that had been associated with his kingship, the talk of usurpation, the talk about the fate of his nephews, the talk about the murder of his wife to marry his niece. Rumours all. But talk and rumours can damage kingship.

Now he was king anew, those dark rumours had been wiped away.

His army had witnessed the whole process.

They knew who the rightful king of England was. Now they would have to shed their blood in order to keep that crown on his head.

6:25 AM 22nd August 1485
A short distance from Ambion Hill, Leicestershire
2 hours and 50 minutes until the death of Richard III

Richard and the army had wasted little time after the crowning ceremony.

The camp had not been struck. The crown, the regalia, and the royal baggage cart had remained behind under guard. They would return after the battle.

Word had arrived that Tudor's army had been sighted on the roman road. Nervous chatter spread the word around the camp. Battle was imminent. Prayers were offered in their hundreds.

Richard was satisfied. Everything was proceeding as he had envisaged. The men had been enthralled at the reacting of the coronation. The sins of his past were wiped away. His kingship had been renewed. Now it was important to implement the lessons of battle from his brother that he had been reminding himself of for the past few weeks.

Choose the ground.

Have the sun and wind behind you.

On this beautiful late summer morning there was no wind. But the sun was already starting to feel warm on his neck. His scouts had been out the previous evening and found a suitable piece of ground close to the villages of Dadlington and Stoke Golding. It was protected by marshland at the rear and offered a slight elevated position.

It was a short march; they would be there within the hour.

7:30 AM 22nd August 1485

Richard III's Position - Close to the villages of Stoke Golding and Darlington , Leicestershire

1 hour and 45 minutes until the death of Richard III

Richard III was at his chosen ground and for the first time he could see his enemy.

He was glad of it. If there was one thing that Richard feared, it was an enemy that he could not see.

Tudor's forces were still at a distance where he could not identify the banners being flown. But he had an idea of the size of the force. He knew straight away that all reports were correct. Despite the defections, he still had the far superior force.

Just as the scouts had reported, the ground on which he had decided to give battle was ideal. It was wide enough for his superior numbers to work to his advantage. The incline was only slight but it was significant enough. There was a slight ridge on which Brackenbury was already assembling the ordnance. There was protection towards the rear were an area of marsh prevented an attack. The slightly lower ground that Tudor would be forced to occupy was narrower due the presence of another area of marshland near the village called Stoke Golding.

Richard would allow Tudor to advance on him and then unleash Brackenbury's guns to do their worst. Never had more ordnance been assembled on a field of battle, and Richard was intrigued to see its effectiveness. Behind the ordnance he arranged his archers. The slight height advantage would give them the ability to fire farther than Tudor’s own Welsh longbow men.

When the time came, Norfolk, a veteran of many conflicts, would command the vanguard and Northumberland, with his four thousand, the rear guard. But at present they were both at Richard’s side as they watched Brackenbury’s men light braziers behind their guns.

Northumberland’s attention was taken by movement behind the trees close to the village of Stoke Golding. Horses. Men. Banners.

“Your Grace,” Northumberland said pointing into the distance.

Richard’s eyes followed Northumberland’s finger and saw for himself.

The Stanleys had arrived.

7:45 AM 22nd August 1485
Richard III's Centre -Close to the villages of Stoke Golding and Darlington , Leicestershire
1 hour and 30 minutes until the death of Richard III

Richard had watched the movement of the Stanley forces for the last fifteen minutes. He had hoped that they would continue their route and join the rest of his men. It was a slim hope, he knew, but he couldn't help but to feel a kick in his stomach as the men –he estimated some five thousand – halted their march on the slight hill in front of the village of Stoke Golding.

The only positive he could draw was that Stanley did not seem to be planning on joining Tudor's forces that had drawn ever closer.

Richard gazed out towards the advancing army and could just about make out the principle banners. He made mental notes of the traitors. If they survived the carnage that would shortly be unleashed, then they would suffer more. They had been playing this game for nigh on thirty years. Richard vowed that when he was victorious his people would never again rise up against their king. England needed to be as one. The only way for that to happen was for the last remaining Lancastrian heir to be slain.

But Tudor would have to wait for his death for a while. He was still almost a mile away and at the present time Richard had business with Lord Thomas Stanley and his brother.

He demanded parchment and a quill. He hurriedly scratched a message and gave it to his quickest rider.

He looked at Norfolk and raised his eyes, “I hope for Strange’s sake we shall get a positive reply.”

The stare that Norfolk returned suggested that he strongly doubted it.

7:54 AM 22nd August 1485

Lord Stanley's Position - Just Outside Stoke Golding, Leicestershire

1 hour and twenty one minutes until the death of Richard III

Richard's message was being read carefully by Lord Thomas Stanley.

The king had dressed it up with some flowery language and made a few efforts at gracious pleasantry but the tone of the message was blunt.

It essentially said one thing.

Bring your men into my battle lines now. Failure to comply will result in the immediate execution of your son.

Despite the circumstances Thomas Stanley thought it was a sublime piece of kingship. Richard was just the sort of king that his brother had been, and his father would have been before them, given the opportunity. It was pure brinkmanship. It was harsh. It was ruthless.

It was how a king should act.

Truth be told it almost swayed him. Not because of the consequences, but because he knew that Richard was the ideal king.

Stanley thought about his son and his heir. He must have known when he rode off on his father's instructions from Nottingham to join Richard's forces that he would be used as pawn in this deadly game. Thomas' mind drifted back to his son's birth. The news that his wife had delivered a son was one of the greatest feelings of his life. He got blind drunk for the next two days to celebrate. He would never forget holding the little helpless child in his arms for the first time. His mind came forward a little in time and he recalled his son's first little set of armour and how thrilled he had been to receive it. Stanley would watch for hours as the young boy went through training in swordsmanship in the yard with his tutors. He always was an intelligent boy and he had taken to his academic studies well; he had particularly excelled in Greek. When he was just fourteen his father had been away at court and the boy had negotiated a settlement with some of the tenants on what could have turned into a very disagreeable and sustained dispute. Stanley had been very impressed when he had received a letter from him telling him about it.

Strange was a boy to be proud of. He was a fine heir and would take the name of Stanley and do great things with it. Thomas was sure of it.

The king knew he had the upper hand. He knew of Thomas' affection for the man. The life of a man's son was the ultimate bargaining tool.

Stanley was only too aware that Richard would carry out his threat if provoked. Over the years Richard had been schooled well in the art of ruthlessness. He had witnessed the orders his brother Edward had calmly given after the battle at Tewksbury. All the Lancastrian lords were pulled out of the abbey and executed without trial. Those that wouldn't come were simply struck down in the nave. Blood stained the abbey floor and the place had to be re-consecrated after the massacre. Richard had been present at his brother's side in the Tower when they had returned victorious from battle and the order had been issued to murder the witless old King Henry in his bed. He had seen his brother sign the execution warrant of their other brother, Clarence, and authorise his drowning in a butt of malmsey wine.

Richard had learnt that kings had to be ruthless if they wanted to survive. It was ingrained in him from years of bloody battles.

Stanley remembered that fateful day in the Tower of London. The council meeting where Richard, then Lord Protector, launched his bid for the throne. Richard had left the meeting in a gracious mood to satisfy a whim for some strawberries. Yet he returned later in a foul temper shouting treason. Before he knew it, he himself was incarcerated and accused of unspeakable things. Yet he thought himself fortunate that he didn't meet the same fate as his friend Hastings. His execution without trial on a block of wood was the sort of move that Richard's brother would have made. Quick. Efficient. Ruthless. Then there were the boys. Indeed, Stanley shivered for a moment thinking about the two young princes. Actually, the young king and his brother. When he was released and elevated back into favour he became Constable of the Tower. One of the first things he did was search for any trace of the boys. There was none.

Of course this proved nothing.

But just like his brother, Richard was uncompromising and he was ruthless. He was a king.

However, Thomas Stanley knew that Richard III of England was not the only one on the battlefield that morning that could be ruthless.

Stanley leant towards the king's messenger and whispered a short reply in his ear. The messenger's eyes grew wide at the response.

"You understand?" Stanley demanded of the messenger.

"Yes My Lord," agreed the man.

"Then ride to your king," Stanley instructed.

As he watched the messenger ride off, he flicked a single tear from his cheek.

8:00 AM 22nd August 1485
St Margret's Church, Stoke Golding, Leicestershire

1 hour and fifteen minutes until the death of Richard III

Edward Fisher rushed up the stone stairs of the church tower.

Word had quickly spread around the village that the armies of King Richard and that of the Welshmen were to meet on the marshy plains below. Fear was in the air. Armies plundered wherever they went: they cared nothing for the farmers' crops, the brewers' ale, or the fathers' daughters.

In times of fear and crisis there was only one place that people assembled. Their church.

Edward Fisher was a young man, a hunter, and it was widely accepted that he had some of the sharpest eyes in the village. As most of the villagers had abandoned their work for the day to pray for safety, they voted Edward Fisher to be one of those to climb the tower to watch and report on the proceedings.

Fisher blinked as the bright sunlight hit him, climbing out onto the roof of the tower. He was stunned at the sight that met him when his eyes finally adjusted. There were thousands of men assembled below, in what appeared to be three great armies. Once the shock had passed, he reported the phenomenal sight. The sunlight glinted off the metal armour and swords, and he could see a great sea of banners and standards too far away for even his eyes to make out the markings.

He found himself a comfortable position and settled down for the greatest view of the greatest show he would ever see.

8:02 AM 22nd August 1485

The Cistercian Abby at Merevale, near Atherstone

One hour and thirteen minutes until the death of Richard III

Jasper Tudor prayed on his knees.

He would much rather be in his saddle charging into battle. But his nephew had given him this task and he knew that it was one he must accept.

He hadn't given much thought to how he might manage to get the Lady Margret out of the country. He hoped that it wouldn't come to that.

Instead he hoped that he would be escorting the King's Mother down to London.

Time would tell what his task would be.

He prayed a little harder.

8:09 AM 22nd August 1485

Richard III's centre - Close to the villages of Stoke Golding and Dadlington, Leicestershire

1 hour and six minutes until the death of Richard III

"I have other sons."

Richard had made the messenger repeat Lord Stanley's words back to him for a second time.

There was no doubt. Stanley was refusing the king's orders. He was sacrificing his own son. Richard, who had gone through the pain of losing a son, could scarcely believe it. "I have other sons." No doubt a weakly concealed barb.

Anger grew in Richard's body. Stanley was a traitor. Just like that venomous wife of his.

But there was something strange about the behaviour of the Stanley forces. Something that made little sense. He looked over towards them. They were clearly set into two groups. The banners made them easy to identify. There were the forces of Thomas Stanley himself, stood closest to the village. Then a short way further down the slope were the forces of his brother Sir William Stanley.

Neither group was making an attempt to join with the forces of Tudor.

Richard was unsure what he was dealing with.

Was it simply the case that even at this late hour the Stanleys had yet to decide which side they were to support? Replaying the message from Stanley in his mind. It was hardly definitive. He was simply responding to the threat to execute Strange. He didn't state that he would be standing against the king. The Stanleys certainly had a long standing reputation of trying to play for both sides. Could it be that they would wait to see which way the battle would swing before lending their support?

Was it possible that Stanley might join him in battle?

If that were the case would then the execution of Strange force Stanley's hand and ensure he fought with Tudor?

Richard had a decision to make.

8:17 AM 22nd August 1485
Richard III's centre - Close to the villages of Stoke Golding and Dadlington, Leicestershire
Fifty Eight minutes until the death of Richard III

Richard had agonised over his decision for a full five minutes.

Neither Norfolk nor Northumberland were asked for advice and neither offered it willing. They both knew that this was a decision that Richard had to make alone.

Richard watched Tudor's men fall into line. The Earl of Oxford's banner was proudly flying in the heart of the vanguard. Tudor's own Welsh Dragon was fluttering limply at the rear. It would seem that Tudor would not be leading his quest for the crown himself. It made sense. Why would Tudor command the forces when he had an experienced man like Oxford in his ranks? He glanced over at the banners of Rhys Ap Thomas. One word leapt to his mind: Traitor. Like so many other long dead kings of England he couldn't trust the Welsh. He recognised some of the other banners, and the presence of Sir Richard Corbett's shocked him – he had thought him a loyal man. Retributions would be made in time, but at present he had a battle to win.

In amongst the sea of banners one significant one was missing, the banner of Jasper Tudor. It made little sense that the man who had done so much to get Henry Tudor on this battlefield wasn't present at the end. He has probably chosen to flee like the dog he is, thought Richard. He has probably worked out that this is a hopeless cause and is now more concerned with saving his own neck while his nephew gave his. He is probably riding for the coast will all haste.

Yet he was worried by this absence. Was there a trick about to be played somewhere? Time after time he had witnessed his brother attack by surprise and win decisive victories. Was Jasper Tudor currently behind a similar surprise attack? He summoned the scouts and gave out orders that they were to seek out the possibility of another army. If Jasper Tudor attacked from the rear, then he would be trapped on three sides.

His eyes drifted towards the Stanleys. They stood passively waiting for matters to play out.

The decision had to be made about Strange.

Richard was a king. He had to act like one. His order to Stanley had been blatantly refused. It was the culmination of weeks of dissent from Stanley. It mattered not that the man had not yet appeared to have joined Tudor's forces. He had to be ruthless. The threat he had made had to be carried out.

He issued the order to execute Lord Strange without a trace of regret.

8:30 AM 22nd August 1485

Richard III's centre - Close to the villages of Stoke Golding and Dadlington, Leicestershire

Forty five minutes until the death of Richard III

Richard was in command of his centre.

Norfolk and Northumberland had ridden over to command their respective battle groups.

Engagement with the enemy was imminent.

However, there was one more piece of theatre that needed to be played out.

Richard's herald had ridden to the middle ground and stood impassively waiting.

After a moment's pause the Earl of Oxford, with two bodyguards, rode out to meet him.

Richard smiled. What did Oxford think was going to happen? Did he think his herald would disobey the laws of chivalry? For a moment his mind flicked back to Tewkesbury and the Lancastrians being pulled out the Abby to be butchered by his brother's men. On reflection maybe Oxford had reason to be wary after all.

From his elevated position, Richard knew this whole process was futile, yet it had to be done. The herald was offering terms to Oxford. Terms that weren't particularly favourable. Terms that Richard knew would be rejected.

The entire conversation took less than two minutes. In the end Oxford shook his head and turned away.

A battle it would be. Richard was not surprised. Nor was he disappointed.

8:32 AM 22nd August 1485

Richard III's centre - Close to the villages of Stoke Golding and Dadlington, Leicestershire

Forty three minutes until the death of Richard III

Sir William Harrington saw the Earl of Oxford shake his head and knew that battle would soon begin.

He approached Richard, who urged him to speak swiftly.

"Your Grace, I have your order to behead my Lord Strange," began Harrington. "Yet battle approaches, Your Grace. Your vanguard shall soon be engaged. My position is here. If the deed is done now it shall be a badly conceived affair, without presence of priest." He looked over towards the Stanley positions on the hill. "We shall have them soon on the field — the father, the uncle, and the son, all three. Then you may deem with your mouth what kind of death that they shall die."

Richard was only too aware that battle was imminent — this was the reason for the order in the first place. Anger rose that his orders were being questioned. Yet at the same time he found that Harrington had a valid point. He fought to control his temper. Calm heads were required at this hour.

Then he saw Tudor ride from his place at the rear, his standard bearer at his side. He rode down the front line, on occasion pausing to speak to an individual.

Interesting, thought Richard.

As he watched he turned swiftly to Harrington, “You have your orders Sir William.”

Harrington showed no emotion, simply nodding and turning to carry out his grisly task.

8:33 AM 22nd August 1485

Henry Tudor's Vanguard - Close to the villages of Stoke Golding and Dadlington, Leicestershire

Forty two minutes until the death of Richard III

Henry Tudor rode down his line with a determined smile on his face.

He did not ride swiftly; he wanted his men to see him. He shouted out encouraging words as he went. On occasion he stopped and spoke to an individual whose face he recalled. It mattered not to him if the man he spoke to was a knight, a gentleman, or a common man. It mattered neither if he were English, Welsh, Scottish, French, or Breton. All were needed since Stanley had chosen not to fulfill his promise of yesterday.

He knew that if he were to wear the crown of England this day then his men would have to fight like dogs. The men would have to do it without Stanley's aid. He was going to give them all the encouragement that they needed.

"Bring me this usurper and reward a plenty you shall have," thundered Tudor to no one in particular. His cry was met with a roar of approval from the men of Rhys Ap Thomas, whom he was close to at the time.

Tudor paused and soaked in the adoration of his men.

If this was what it were like to be a king then it would be a glorious thing.

8:37 AM 22nd August 1485

Richard III's Centre - Close to the villages of Stoke Golding and Dadlington, Leicestershire

Thirty seven minutes until the death of Richard III

Richard had no intention of making the first move. He held the higher ground. Only just barely, but higher ground it was. He would wait for Oxford to advance on him.

He watched as a messenger was sent from Oxford's front line to Tudor now in position again at the rear, a small squadron of men at his side. After a brief conversation the messenger return to Oxford.

It was the final order to attack.

Slowly Oxford advanced forward.

The stages of battle always fascinated Richard. At this point matters were slow, calm, and orderly. It was akin to the opening moves of a game of chess. There was a comforting familiarity about them. There was time to muse, just as he was doing now. Yet once the forces actually engaged, nothing was orderly. A battle was chaos. Pure bloody chaos. Anything could happen – and it normally did.

Richard immediately noticed that Oxford had not spilt his forces. A prudent move, thought Richard, why spilt an inferior force?

Richard raised his arm.

As they came into range Richard's arm fell and the largest collection of ordnance ever assembled on a battlefield was unleashed.

The sound was deafening. Smoke filled the air, the smell of gunpowder hit the nostrils and shot tore mercilessly into Oxford's right flank.

The massacre had begun.

8:40 AM 22nd August 1485

The Earl of Oxford's Battle Line - Close to the villages of Stoke Golding and Dadlington, Leicestershire

Thirty five minutes until the death of Richard III

Oxford knew that the first blast from the cannon would be the worst. Now that the first volley had been fired he had a few minutes while the barrels cooled and the gunners reloaded.

He could hear screams from his flank where the shot had hit. Shot could rip limbs from bodies without the person even realising it for a moment. Clearly now his injured men realised it.

Shouts from that same flank drew his attention and he immediately saw a problem. The ground was wet and boggy, almost marsh-like, and the first line of men were struggling. If they continued they would be easy targets for the gunners and archers. He immediately gave the order to wheel.

This would benefit him two-fold. Not only would the troops have firm ground on which to advance, but they would be offered protection from the gunfire.

He watched as his men completed the manoeuvre. Another explosion from the ridge signaled the next volley from the cannon. Fortunately, as he predicted, it proved far less devastating than the first.

But just as the ringing in ears from the cannon had ceased, there was a new sound to strike fear into the hearts of his men. The noise of a thousand shrill whistles.

Richard's archers had fired.

8:43AM 22nd August 1485
Richard III's Centre - Close to the villages of Stoke Golding and Dadlington, Leicestershire
Thirty two minutes until the death of Richard III

Fifteen hundred archers produced a glorious sight.

So long as you stood behind them.

Stand on the receiving side and they produced the sight of incoming death.

Richard watched the arrows soar into the air like early summer swallows. They seemed to pause for a moment at their zenith before curving gracefully into a deadly dive.

Some of the arrows fell uselessly into the earth.

Some of the arrows hit armour or shield and bounced broken into the mud.

But some struck flesh. Injuring. Blinding. Maiming. Killing.

Oxford's advance staggered for a moment before his archers responded with their own deadly hail storm.

For Richard, his view of arrows was now no longer such a glorious sight. He watched as his own men fell because of death dropping from the sky.

Oxford drove his men forward, keen to get them all through the marshy area as quickly as possible.

Volley after volley of arrows were exchanged. The only sounds that men heard were the whistles of the arrows, their own laboured breathing, and the screams from the injured and dying.

And then Norfolk moved Richard's vanguard forward to engage with Oxford and his advancing troops.

8:45AM 22nd August 1485
Richard III's Rear - Close to the villages of Stoke Golding and Dadlington, Leicestershire
Thirty minutes until the death of Richard III

Sir William Harrington had reached Richard's rear, under the command of Northumberland. He was not too ashamed to say he had flinched in his saddle when the guns roared into life. Never in his life had he heard such a sound. He had broken into a canter as he heard the death whistle of the arrows. It would be pointless to die due to a stray arrow.

He could not believe what he had been ordered to do.

As he rode closer Northumberland looked at him inquiringly, wondering if Harrington had brought an order from the king for him. Harrington simply shook his head, "I am to be the king's executioner, so help me God."

Northumberland could not help but to cross himself, "He is behind the lines. At the baggage cart. May God have mercy on his soul." He then turned his attention back to the exchanges below.

Harrington rode on, past the line of men who all followed his progress with desperate, worried eyes. He looked over to the Stanley position by Stoke Golding and could not comprehend how a man could abandon his son like this. Had Stanley joined Richard's forces, they would have been unassailable and Strange would not be in this position. What kind of a man was Stanley? He had not even joined the forces of his step-son. He might have been able to understand the man's motives more if he had done so. No doubt Tudor would have offered him the earth for his support. But he just stood there, not committed to either side, simply content to let matters play out in front of him while Richard carried out his threat. It made little sense.

He had no trouble finding the carts Northumberland had mentioned. The logistics of battle were normally just as important as the fighting itself. An army could not march without water or food. Shot had to be transported for the ordnance. The archers could fire twelve arrows a minute. A stockpile of arrows where required. A battle could easily be lost due to poorly planned logistics. But Richard was experienced. What was not required for the battle had been left behind on Ambion Hill. The essentials for fighting were brought on the carts.

Strange was tied crudely to the wheel of one cart, whilst two beggarly looking men stood guard over him. Harrington could not help but think that he wouldn't have put those two in charge of his daughter's puppy. Strange looked a pitiful sight. He was dressed in his armour as though he were a still a valued member of Richard's forces and not the king's prisoner; the son of a traitor whose actions had cost his heir his life.

Sir William drew his sword. Strange saw him approach and knew this was it. His father had finally abandoned him in the quest for a greater glory. He had moments left to live. He closed his eyes and began to pray.

Strange's captors exchanged nervous looks as Harrington drew closer.

"I come with the king's orders," he said forcefully. "You men are dismissed."

The men stood there unsure of what to do.

"Go, fools. You do not want to witness this act." Harrington demand as he raised his sword.

Harrington was an imposing sight and the captors turned on their heels and fled towards the safety of Northumberland's lines.

Strange knew what was coming. It took him all of his effort to force his knees not to buckle. He wondered what death would be like. He hoped there would be no pain. He recited the Lord's Prayer aloud, determined that the Lord would receive his soul when the fatal blow came. He would be in paradise soon enough.

Harrington felt sickened to his stomach. This was no just and rightful execution. The man about to die had done the king no ill. He felt he had been ordered to commit murder in the king's name. These were not the actions of a knight.

As he drew closer he could almost smell the fear on Strange's shallow breath. He felt nothing but pity. And in a moment he made his decision. He would not burn in hell for this act of abomination.

Harrington turned and looked behind him. Northumberland was obscured by his own lines and all of those men's attentions were taken by the battle unfolding in front of him.

He raised his sword and instead of bringing it down on Strange's neck he used to slice through the bonds that held him. “You will receive no death by my hand, my Lord.”

Strange opened his eyes, stunned. “Sir William?”

“Go, my Lord. I will not be party to this.” Harrington pointed to the right, “Your father stands over there. Take a horse from the baggage train and ride to him if you wish. Traitorous rogue that he is. And when you see him, I would not blame you for thrusting a dagger into the man’s venomous belly.”

“I do not understand,” replied Strange, perplexed that he was not yet dead.

“Neither do I, my Lord,” agreed Harrington. “Neither do I.”

8:47AM 22nd August 1485
St Margret's Church Stoke Golding Leicestershire
Twenty Eight minutes until the death of Richard III

Edward Fisher watched the arrows fly and physically shivered: even at this distance he could see that the air was thick with them like a flock of starlings dancing in formation.

He imagined what it was like to stand under that barrage of fire and decided that it was something that he never wanted to do.

He felt sick, hundreds of men even now must lie dead or injured.

He didn't feel like watching any longer but for some strange reason he couldn't take his eyes off the destruction that played out in front of him.

8:52AM 22nd August 1485
Richard III's Centre - Close to the villages of Stoke Golding and Dadlington, Leicestershire
Twenty three minutes until the death of Richard III

Richard watched as Norfolk's troops engaged in hand-to-hand fighting with Oxford's.

The ordnance and arrows had stopped. For those firing it was impossible to differentiate between one's own side and the enemies. It made little sense for Richard to order a volley of shot to be fired into Norfolk's own flanks.

It was clear almost immediately that Oxford's men would not buckle and fold from Norfolk's attack. In fact, a number of Norfolk's men were disengaging from the rear ranks and were turning to flee. The mercenaries who fought on Oxford's front line were skilled, experienced fighting men. They held the line as the forces initially clashed and they counter attacked after the energy of their enemies faltered.

The fact that Oxford had not split his forces into the traditional battle groups was playing to his advantage and the fact that he had inferior numbers mattered little.

It was clear that Norfolk needed support. Richard looked down the line of his centre towards Sir Robert Brackenbury and waved him forward. Brackenbury lowered his visor and advanced with over two thirds of Richard's centre.

Richard's wary eyes glanced over to the Stanleys. Nothing had changed. They were still as impassive as they were an hour ago. He knew their involvement could well prove to be decisive.

One way or the other.

8:55AM 22nd August 1485

Rhys Ap Thomas' position on the battle line - Close to the villages of Stoke Golding and Dadlington, Leicestershire

Twenty minutes until the death of Richard III

Rhys Ap Thomas knew exactly what was expected of him and his men.

He had spent many hours in recent days with the Earl of Oxford discussing military strategy. Thomas conceded that, for an Englishman, Oxford's plans for the battle were sound. He had been prudent enough to devise a number of strategies depending on the number of men at his disposal. Stanley's failure to live up to his promise to join their ranks had meant that Oxford had kept his men together as one battle group. He was insistent that the line had to be held. He had been defeated by Norfolk many years ago at Barnett because of the failure of his men to hold the line. The order had been issued as they advanced that no man was to move more than ten feet away from their respective standard.

Oxford was at the far right of their line and Thomas to the left.

Thomas' job was to punch a hole through Norfolk's line so that their enemy could become encircled.

Slowly his best men formed into a tightly packed wedge formation. Compact, strong, and with a tip designed to break their opponent's line.

Thomas issued the order to push the wedge forward.

As expected Norfolk's men broke.

8:58AM 22nd August 1485

Richard III's Centre - Close to the villages of Stoke Golding and Dadlington, Leicestershire

Eighteen minutes until the death of Richard III

Richard watched in disbelief as Brackenbury and his men added to Norfolk's numbers but failed to break Oxford's lines.

Rhys Ap Thomas' banner was at the heart of the fighting and yet again Richard felt betrayal and anger.

The king took another cursory glance over towards the slopes of Stoke Golding. There was still no movement from the Stanleys. What price would he pay for those six thousand men now.

The fighting was bloody and brutal. Men lay on the ground injured, but were trampled to death from the weight of the men leaping to take their place in the line. The groans of the dying were almost louder than the sound of blade on blade.

Slowly, very slowly, Richard could see that Oxford's men were gaining ground. Thomas' men had formed into a wedge and were punching through Norfolk's line.

Something had to be done.

He called the messenger and gave him orders to race to Northumberland.

Norfolk and Brackenbury needed support. He had planned to leave Northumberland to counter the threat of the Stanleys. But that threat would prove irrelevant if Oxford's men broke through.

Northumberland needed to engage.

8:59AM 22nd August 1485

Lord Stanley's Position - Just Outside Stoke Golding, Leicestershire

16 minutes until the death of Richard III

Stanley still could not tell which way the battle would go. Tudor's men had clearly gained ground.

But to Stanley it seemed that, as soon as Northumberland attacked, Tudor's forces would be overwhelmed.

Whatever his step-son had promised him, he would not risk joining a losing side. At present he needed to wait.

Then he saw a lone horsemen approaching directly from Richard's rear.

His heart sank. Another messenger with probably another order to disobey. Or worse, news of the execution of his son.

9:00AM 22nd August 1485
Richard III's Centre - Close to the villages of Stoke Golding and Dadlington, Leicestershire
Fifteen minutes until the death of Richard III

Richard looked along his lines to Northumberland.

The man sat on his horse as impassively as the Stanleys over by the village.

Why in the name of God wasn't the man moving forward?

Richard looked back towards the fighting. Norfolk's lines were buckling and more men of his were fleeing the field. The line needed reinforcements now.

The king looked back at Northumberland and waved him forward in a desperate gesture.

Still Northumberland did not move.

Richard was confused.

Then horror overcame him as the realisation hit.
This was treachery.

Northumberland had betrayed him.

9:01AM 22nd August 1485
Richard III's Rear - Close to the villages of Stoke Golding and Dadlington, Leicestershire
Fourteen minutes until the death of Richard III

"My Lord of Northumberland? You heard the king's order?" questioned the messenger when it became obvious that Northumberland wasn't moving his men forward.

The messenger saw the break in Norfolk's lines himself and saw Richard's desperate wave. Yet still Northumberland did nothing.

"My Lord? The king needs you."

"I heard the goddamn order you fool," snapped back Northumberland with a glare that could kill.

The venom in Northumberland's reply stunned the young messenger. Yet he held his composure, "You wish to return a message to His Grace my lord?"

The silence from Northumberland was deafening.

The messenger waited for a few seconds, then shook his head and rode off back to report to Richard.

Northumberland stared impassively at the battle line and watched as Norfolk's men were overrun.

9:03AM 22nd August 1485
Richard III's Centre - Close to the villages of Stoke Golding and Dadlington, Leicestershire
Twelve minutes until the death of Richard III

Norfolk's men were losing ground slowly and becoming overwhelmed. Brackenbury's forces had only delayed the process.

Richard had a bitter taste in his mouth. It was a taste that he had known before and a taste that he had never wanted to experience again.

It was the taste of defeat.

Northumberland's men could have held the line. Not only held it, but four thousand fresh troops would have ran through Oxford's line.

Richard could not fathom the treachery. Why? Why bother to rouse the troops? Why march from the North? Why report as ordered to Leicester? Why take part in the coronation re-enactment? Why did he sit on his horse next to him not one hour ago offering advice with Norfolk? It was inexplicable.

Juan de Salazar approached Richard and offered his advice, "Sire, take measure to put your personal safety beyond doubt. Treason has been played against you this day. Take a swift horse and your few trusted men and flee this field."

Richard stared at de Salazar like a lost man, stunned that it had come to this. Then Richard's attention was seized, and he could scarcely believe what he was seeing.

Tudor had ceased moving forward with Oxford's advances. Oxford's wheel manoeuvre to avoid the marsh and ordnance, when combined with the rapid gain in ground, had left Richard a clear, unobstructed path to him.

He just sat there, exposed, with a small contingent of what? One hundred? One hundred and twenty men at most?

It was the error of an inexperienced commander. And on a battlefield, errors cost lives.

Now Richard had a different taste in his mouth.

Hope.

If he killed Tudor, nothing else would matter. Not Norfolk's broken line. Not Northumberland's treachery. Not Stanley's passivity. The battle that was playing out in front of him would become irrelevant. If Tudor perished, Richard would remain King of England.

Richard felt the adrenaline surge in his body. He would do what he did best. He would fight in battle and he would retain his crown… Or he would die in the process.

"Salazar," Richard said to the man that had been addressing him. "In God's name I will not yield a single step. This day I will die a king or, more likely, taste victory."

He reached down to his valet at his side and took his battle axe in his hand. His gauntleted fist came up and pulled down his visor.

Richard raised his arm and held it the air. After a moments pause he brought it down in a dramatic manner.

As one his men sprang forward.

To death or glory.

And the King of England led the charge.

9:04AM 22nd August 1485

Henry Tudor's Position - Close to the villages of Stoke Golding and Dadlington, Leicestershire

Eleven minutes until the death of Richard III

Sir John Cheyney first spotted the threat and shouted a warning.

Lewes Ap Griffith looked up and saw the cavalry charging down towards them, three or four hundred strong. Fear knotted his stomach. He knew that they would be overrun.

Cheyney rode up aside Tudor. "Dismount Sire," he advised. "Do not make yourself an easy target."

Tudor took a final glance at the horsemen charging towards them and he saw at the centre a knight with a circle of gold about his head. The realisation struck him: Richard himself was coming to kill him.

Tudor did what he was instructed and dove into the protection of his men.

"Protect his Grace at all costs," bellowed the giant form of Cheyney who was still on his massive warhorse.

The troops compressed into a square to offer one another as much protection as possible. They knew they were on their own: Oxford was too far advanced to send back reinforcements, if he had even noticed what was happening.

They had to keep the square.

They had to protect Henry Tudor.

But they still had one final die to cast.

9:05AM 22nd August 1485
Lord Stanley's Position - Just Outside Stoke Golding, Leicestershire
Ten minutes until the death of Richard III

Lord Thomas Stanley could scarcely believe it. The horseman had not been a messenger from the king: it had been his son.

Strange did not take Sir William Harrington's advice to plunge a dagger into the stomach of his father. Instead, he embraced him. He knew the position his father was in. It was almost impossible. His wife's son was facing the king in battle and had requested his support. Tudor had promised him titles, offices of State, and lands that would make the Stanleys the most formidable family in England.

Yet even with such an offer, his father had not thrown his lot in with his step-son. He could not, for Strange was the king's prisoner.

Strange hurriedly told his father of Harrington's refusal of Richard's order and how he had been released. Stanley had not been surprised the order to execute Strange had been issued. But he was surprised that it hadn't been carried out. It told him that there was dissent in Richard's ranks.

He looked over to the battle and could not determine why Northumberland had not yet engaged. Surely Richard had ordered his advance. Possibly the marsh was wider that it appeared, preventing him from advancing on Oxford's position without a time-consuming and futile flanking manoeuvre. Or possible it was something else?

Possibly Northumberland had refused to engage. Tudor had told him that he had been in communication with the Earl…

Sudden cries from his men got his attention and he saw what they were watching.

A force of horseman, three or four hundred strong were charging down the slope from Richard's line. And then he saw it. The White Boar standard. The flash of gold on a helmet. Richard had committed himself to battle.

He turned his head to see their target and he froze. Tudor had lagged too far behind Oxford's line and was terribly exposed. He saw that Tudor had seen the danger as well and his men were scrambling to form a defensive position.

Stanley immediately knew that nothing else mattered. This was a battle within a battle. Whoever won this encounter would emerge victorious. This battle was simply about the opposing commanders, and if one died then the battle was over. The other would be the victor and have the right to wear the crown of England. From Stanley's position it looked almost beyond doubt that Richard would be victorious.

He thought quickly. Matters had changed swiftly in seconds. His son was safe and outside of Richard's control. He no longer had that burden hanging over his head. Richard may well have overwhelming numbers to defeat Tudor's bodyguards. But with the defensive position they had taken, it would take some time. Richard had four hundred men at most. His brother had three thousand mounted horses.

He issued the orders for his brother to defend Tudor.

9:06AM 22nd August 1485
Henry Tudor's Position - Close to the villages of Stoke Golding and Dadlington, Leicestershire
Nine minutes until the death of Richard III

Richard's cavalry line drew closer and everyone standing within Tudor's protective square could see the king clearly. Richard had been overtaken by some of his men, but he remained in the centre just behind his banner.

Tudor's men were about to throw their last die.

Just before the cavalry crashed into them, a row of French pike men knelt and raised their formidable eighteen-foot long pikes.

Many on the front line of Richard's forces were unhorsed as their beasts impaled themselves on the spikes.

Richard saw the pikes raise and managed to slow his steed enough to prevent himself from meeting the same fate as many of his men. He assessed the situation for a moment. The pike men had done their job; they had slowed Richard's attack. But now most of them were useless – some had broken pikes, while others still had impaled horses or knights on their weapons. And there were so few of them.

His charge had been slowed, but it had not been halted.

Shouting words of encouragement to his men, Richard spurred his horse forward. Such was the force of the animal that it brushed aside the man in front of him. And before he knew it he was in amongst Tudor's men. He raised his axe and brought it down on the first figure he could see. He heard a crack as it broke the man's skull, killing him in an instant.

Richard's men saw their king in amongst the enemy and leapt forward to assist him. Some are pulled from their horses and are dispatched with a sword blade through the visor. Others are unseated, but rise up and fight. Still others remain on horse and thrust downwards with axe and sword.

It is carnage.

9:07AM 22nd August 1485

Sir William Stanley's position- Close to the villages of Stoke Golding and Dadlington, Leicestershire

Eight minutes until the death of Richard III

Sir William Stanley's men charged forward.

Speed was critical. There was ground to cover and if they didn't cover it swiftly enough then the man they were riding to defend would be dead.

He saw Tudor's pike men slow Richard's charge and he knew that this action would gain them sufficient time to strike.

Although the desired outcome was that Henry Tudor was to live, there was no doubt that, now that Tudor's forces had been committed, Richard had to die. He couldn't imagine the retribution that would come their way if Richard was victorious. As he drove his horse faster his mind played with the fanciful scenario of what would occur if both claimants to the crown perished in this final endgame. Who would the Stanleys support then?

He had no idea.

He prayed that Tudor would hold until they arrived.

9:08AM 22nd August 1485

Henry Tudor's Position - Close to the villages of Stoke Golding and Dadlington, Leicestershire

Seven minutes until the death of Richard III

Richard continued hacking through Tudor's men. He was a man possessed. He could think of nothing but getting to Tudor.

He saw the banner of the Welsh Dragon and knew that Tudor would not be far behind.

He ploughed forward, tearing his way through the bodies that dare to stand in front of him. Blow after blow rained down from his axe, crushing skulls and spilling blood as he went.

And then in a moment the passage in front of him seemed to clear, like Moses parting the Red Sea. And there was Sir William Brandon, the banner of the Welsh Dragon grasped in his gauntlet. Traitorous bastard, thought Richard as he pressed forward.

It was not a fair fight. Brandon's principle concern was to keep Tudor's banner flying.

Richard cut him down with ease.

Henry Tudor's banner fell.

9:09AM 22nd August 1485
Henry Tudor's Position - Close to the villages of Stoke Golding and Dadlington, Leicestershire
Six minutes until the death of Richard III

Henry Tudor watched in horror as Sir William Brandon fell with his banner.

Richard was clearly visible just yards away, his gold circlet sat proudly on his head, defying people to stand against him.

Tudor's forces edged in front of him, attempting to shield him from the king. But it was too late. Richard had seen the man that wanted his crown and he could think of nothing but reaching him and ending this once and for all.

Sir John Cheyney was close to Tudor. He had remained on his horse and he too had seen the banner fall and the danger that Tudor was in. His first reaction was to reach the banner and thrust it skywards again. But despite their significance, banners were just scraps of material sewn by wives and widows. Someone else could handle the fallen standard. Instead, Cheyney positioned his giant frame between Tudor and the king.

Richard had his nemesis in his sight and now his vision had been obscured by the giant man in front of him. It didn't take much thought to determine that it was Cheyney blocking his route.

"Traitor," he shouted in unbridled anger.

Cheyney had always been a Yorkist. He had been his brother's master of the horse. And yet, he had deserted to Tudor's side.

The man was huge, by far the largest knight he had ever seen. But Richard was not going to let that stop him. He was blocking the path to his objective.

He swung his axe at a man who had tried to grab his bridle and hewed the top of his skull clean off. However, such was the force of the blow that his axe flew out of his hand. A horse pulled up alongside him and the man who sat in the saddle was one of his own, alive but injured. The man's visor had been raised and he had an arrow sticking out of his right eye. He looked at Richard with his remaining good eye, but he didn't see him. Richard felt a moment's shame, as he didn't even know the name of this man who was about to die for him. The knight was holding a lance that had been broken about three-quarters of the way up. Without a second thought, Richard took it out of the man's failing grip and then watched him very slowly fall off the far side of the horse.

With the distraction out of the way he looked straight at Cheyney and charged.

9:10AM 22nd August 1485
Henry Tudor's Position - Close to the villages of Stoke Golding and Dadlington, Leicestershire
Five minutes until the death of Richard III

In that one battle charge Richard perfected everything he had been taught since a child.

He sat low in the saddle. He kept his head down. He held the lance, or at least what was left of it, at the correct angle.

Even with his great size Cheyney stood no chance at remaining on his steed when the broken lance hit him square in the chest. He fell towards the ground but his left spur caught in the stirrup. With the shock of losing the great weight of its rider the horse bolted. Cheney was dragged through the carnage away from Richard. Finally, the spur became lose and Cheyney fell to the mud.

He was stunned, shocked but still alive.

Equally as shocked was Richard himself. For such a small man unseating a giant like Cheyney was nothing short of miraculous. The shooting pain in his shoulder told him that he had actually achieved the impossible

Just as he was recovering his bearings and was seeking out Tudor, shouts from behind distracted him.

He turned and froze in horror.

All he could see were horses. Hundreds of them. Thousands even.

And the banner of Sir William Stanley.

9:11AM 22nd August 1485
Henry Tudor's Position - Close to the villages of Stoke Golding and Dadlington, Leicestershire
Four minutes until the death of Richard III

Sir William Stanley darted into Richard III's men.

They had been concentrating so hard on wiping out Tudor's bodyguard as quickly as they could that they had failed to see the approaching Stanley forces. The warning cries went out but it was too late, they were overwhelmed by sheer numbers.

Where Tudor's men had seen no hope, they now knew the tide had turned. Their job now was to keep Henry Tudor alive whilst they allowed Stanley's men to commit a massacre.

A Welsh halberd man named Rhys Ap Maredudd grabbed the fallen Tudor standard and raised it high. A roar went up from Henry's men.

Henry himself was in the middle of a group of loyal men who were prepared to sacrifice themselves before allowing anyone near their Lord.

Richard was not far from them and all eyes were on him. He was fighting like a true king should.

They had seen him hack down Brandon.

They had seen him unhorse Cheyney.

They saw him turn and witness the Stanley forces arriving.

They saw him fall.

Then they saw his men rush to protect him.

They knew the battle was entering its endgame.

9:12AM 22nd August 1485
Henry Tudor's Position - Close to the villages of Stoke Golding and Dadlington, Leicestershire
Three minutes until the death of Richard III

Sir Percival Thirlwall had long since been unhorsed. Yet he had risen to his feet and ensured that he kept Richard's standard flying.

He saw the king fall from his horse and his first reaction was to leap towards him.

Sir Percival was not the only one, others rushed forward to keep their king safe.

But it was Sir Percival that reached Richard first to stand protectively over him. Another man appeared and miraculously he still sat astride his horse. Sir Percival took stock of the situation for a moment and realized that it was simply a matter of time. They were being overrun. But more of Richard's men arrived on foot and helped haul the king to his feet. Strangely, his helmet and the gold circlet remained in place. Then another rider appeared and then another. It was a small force, but they were determined.

Richard knew he was about to make his final stand.

Stanley's men were still carving their way through the bulk of the king's rearguard. The majority of Tudor's men seemed intent on blocking anyone's path to their Lord. Percival spied a brief opportunity.

He ordered the first rider off his horse.

"Your Grace," Percival said, getting his head as close to Richard's as he can. "Take this horse. Flee. There will be another day."

Richard stood impassively as though he didn't understand the words.

"Your Grace," Percival pressed again.

"No, my good Percival," replied Richard, his voice surprisingly strong. "Today I will leave this field as King of England or I will die in that office."

Percival's heart sank. He loved his king like no other. But he knew there could only be one outcome of this action.

With one hand holding the White Boar standard high, he raised his short sword in the other. "For the king!" he cried.

Richard's small body of men answered with one voice, "For the king!"

They all charged towards Henry Tudor.

9:13AM 22nd August 1485

Henry Tudor's Position - Close to the villages of Stoke Golding and Dadlington, Leicestershire

Two minutes until the death of Richard III

Lewes Ap Griffith saw the king's forces charging towards him and braced himself with his halbert ready to strike. He had just watched William Stanley's men ride to their rescue. Like everyone else protecting Henry Tudor they knew that eventually victory might soon be assured. However, despite the obvious victory that Stanley's troops would give them, all could still be lost at the last. If Henry Tudor were to perish then all of this bloodshed would have been for nothing.

In spite of the fear he could not help but to laugh. With all of the many thousands on the battlefield it had come down to this.

Fifteen men against fifteen men.

It seemed almost absurd.

Then Richard's forces hit and Griffith could do nothing but thrust, hack, and try to stay alive. His shoulder received a blow from a sword blade, but he felt nothing. He swung at the man in front of him and knocked him to the ground. In one swift movement Griffith was over the top of him and thrusted down into the man's stomach with the point of his halbert. He watched as the man writhed in agony. He gave the weapon a twist and more blood than he ever thought possible spilled onto the muddy ground. He felt bile rise up in his throat. Battle was a sickening, horrifying thing. He knew that for as long as he lived he never wanted to experience one again. The man writhed one final time and blood dribbled out of his mouth. Griffith couldn't stomach it any longer. He vomited over the dying man.

He looked up and saw yet another sickening sight. Sir Percival Thirlwall had been slower than the rest of Richard's men in the charge. His age, and the weight of the White Boar standard, slowed him down. He was an obvious target. One of Stanley's men galloped behind him and struck him square in the back. The man staggered forward, but didn't fall. But now others were upon him like lions picking out the weak. There was a flurry of flashing sword blades and Sir Percival's legs were hacked away from under him. Griffith saw Sir Percival fall but even then, without his legs, he continued to proudly hold Richard's standard skyward.

Griffith pulled his halbert out of the dead man and at the same time he sensed movement behind him.

In one swift movement he turned and swung his weapon. It struck his assailant on the helmet with such force that it flew off. The man staggered backwards at the blow.

Griffith saw something out of the corner of his eye that made him look twice.

The helmet that he had knocked off his assailant was fitted with a circlet of gold.

As the gold circlet bounced over the mud Sir Percival finally succumbed to the blood loss.

The White Boar standard finally fell.

9:14AM 22nd August 1485

Henry Tudor's Position - Close to the villages of Stoke Golding and Dadlington, Leicestershire

One minute until the death of Richard III

Richard III staggered under the blow. His vision was blurred. His shoulder screamed in agony.

He saw his standard fall. He looked at it, laying in the dirt, torn and blood-stained. He was stunned. How had this happened? How had he been defeated by a bastard Welshmen with an inferior force and no military experience? It wasn't possible.

One of Tudor's men, dressed in his colours, approached and Richard lashed out with his sword keeping him at arm's length.

Then another appeared and another.

He was surrounded.

He saw his gold circlet lying in the mud and the thought crossed his mind that no matter how great the king, they all perished in the end.

Tudor's men were taunting him now but Richard couldn't hear the words. Anger rose in his chest. How dare these common men address him in this manner?

He was the last son of York.
He was their liege Lord.
Their sovereign.

As well as anger, something else swelled in his chest. Pride.

He was his father's son.
He was the brother of the mighty Edward IV.
He was the King of England.

And these men would kneel before him.

He charged at the nearest and rose his sword. But before he could strike he was struck on the head from the rear.

His grip faltered and his sword fell to the ground. Then another blow struck him and another.

Richard III of England feel to his knees.

9:15AM 22nd August 1485

Henry Tudor's Position - Close to the villages of Stoke Golding and Dadlington, Leicestershire

Richard III looked up to the darkening sky and knew this was the end.

He was the last of the sons of York. The line was ended. He had no heir.

He thought that a king should die in his bed with his son at his side ready to receive the ring from his finger.

Instead, he would die here in the dirt surrounded by cruel and wicked men. Strangely he found himself wanting his mother.

He felt guilt.

He felt shame.

He knew he had never been worthy.

Lewes Ap Griffith walked slowly forward, his halbert raised.

Richard glanced up and stared him in the eye with utter contempt. The shame and guilt were gone. He was the King of England once again.

Griffith took a deep breath and drove the halbert forward. The point pierced the king's skull and disappeared into the softness of his brain.

Richard III of England slumped lifeless into the filth of the battlefield.

9:18AM 22nd August 1485
Henry Tudor's Position - Close to the villages of Stoke Golding and Dadlington, Leicestershire
Three minutes after the death of Richard III

The last remaining forces of Richard III were soon swept away by the vastly superior numbers of Sir William Stanley. A handful were taken prisoner after surrendering, but most fought to the end.

When it became clear that Richard's men were dead Henry Tudor sank to knees and gave his thanks to God.

He had won the crown.

Unlike his defeated foe all he personally had to do was parry two blows of a sword and keep himself out of harm's way. It wasn't a glorious way to do it, he reflected. But it was effective.

9:20AM 22nd August 1485

Norfolk's Battle Position - Close to the villages of Stoke Golding and Dadlington, Leicestershire

Five minutes after the death of Richard III

Norfolk was watching from a horse as his battle line was now completely overrun, his forces fleeing from the battlefield in droves.

He had seen Richard's charge and knew that his own battle was now completely irrelevant. All that mattered was what happened down there. He had retreated away from the battle line and watched. He had issued an order for a horse and miraculously one was found.

He had seen the Red Dragon standard fall. And his heart leapt with joy. Then he had seen the treasonous charge of Sir William Stanley and then the rise of the Red Dragon once again. He had seen the White Boar standard fall. He waited. And he waited a little more. Finally, he accepted that the White Boar would not rise again.

It was over.

He turned his horse and fled the battlefield.

9:21 AM 21st August 1485
Latham House
6 minutes after the death of Richard III

Margret Beaufort was in her customary place on her knees at prayer.

Suddenly she felt a wave of spiritual euphoria wash over her. Her heart was filled with a joy that she could not describe.

At that moment she knew.

Her son was victorious.

From this moment on she would style herself The Lady Margret, The King's Mother and she would sign all of her correspondence Margret R.

The House of Lancaster was back on the throne of England and she could not help but cry.

9:25AM 22nd August 1485

Henry Tudor's Position - Close to the villages of Stoke Golding and Dadlington, Leicestershire

Ten minutes after the death of Richard III

"I greet you well, your Grace," said Sir William Stanley as he met Henry Tudor on the battlefield. He decided that he would immediately address Tudor as though he were king. Flattery would get you everywhere, he had once been told.

"Not as well as I greet you, Sir William," said Tudor, clasping the hand of his saviour and offering a wide smile.

"Victory, your Grace," whispered Stanley as he looked around the carnage on the battlefield. "This is what victory looks like." Everywhere he looked were injured men and the bodies of the dead. "England is free from tyranny at last."

Tudor nodded, unsure of how to respond. He was king. How should a king respond?

"We should send a rider to my Lord of Oxford, to tell him of our victory," said Stanley.

"Indeed," agreed Tudor attempting to pull himself together. "And a messenger to your brother."

"Already dispatched, your Grace."

Tudor couldn't help to laugh to himself how Stanley's first reaction was to report back to his brother. They were victorious, the Stanley's had finally supported the right side. There was no need for Thomas Stanley to flee the field.

"A horse. Fetch me a horse," shouted Tudor to no one in particular. It did seem fitting that as the king he should be on a horse at this point. He then looked back at Sir William Stanley," We shall ride to your brother together, Sir William. I have a mind to leave this bloody battlefield behind."

Stanley nodded.

It did not take long for a horse to be found for the new king. And when he mounted, Rhys Ap Maredudd appeared next to him, still holding the Red Dragon standard he had rescued out of Sir William Brandon's dead hand.

Before he rode off, he issued orders that Richard's body be found and brought to him intact.

Sir William laboured a moment behind the king as he rode off, and before he followed he issued another order.

"Make sure you find the bloody crown as well. And bring it with all haste over to my brother. Make sure no roguish bastard pockets it. This is no mere trinket we speak of."

9:30 AM 22nd August 1485
St Margret's Church, Stoke Golding, Leicestershire
Fifteen minutes after the death of Richard III

Edward Fisher climbed down the tower of the church. The battle, he believed, is over. However, he cannot determine who has won. The villagers would have to wait for news.

Now was the most dangerous time for the villagers. The injured would soon arrive to seek care. Others would want ale and food.

After they learnt that the battle was finished many people began leaving the church.

They made their way back to their homes and barricaded themselves in.

They hoped that the those seeking help would pass them by.

9:45 AM 22nd August 1485
Dadlington Windmill, Dadlington, Leicestershire
Thirty minutes after the death of Richard III

Norfolk rode wearily towards the windmill. He knew he had to be careful. He could not afford to be captured by Tudor's forces – he doubted that the man would show any compassion.

A voice from behind the stone walls of the windmill shouted out "Father, is that you?"

Norfolk recognised the voice immediately: it was his son the Earl of Surrey. Surrey had been fighting in Norfolk's line but it had been a while since he had seen his banner on the battlefield. Norfolk had worried that his heir had perished. But he also knew they had this arrangement.

They had quickly spied the windmill that morning. Along with the Church at Stoke Golding, it was one of the only prominent landmarks. They had agreed that if the tide turned against them they would meet together here and then they would make their escape to their lands in East Anglia. What was to come after then, they did not know.

Norfolk felt a wave of relief. Losing children was a fact of life, but he certainly had affection for his heir. He kicked his horse and cantered around the far side of the Windmill.

Norfolk froze.

His son was certainly alive. But he was on his knees his hands bound and a sword held to his throat.

Men appeared from the shadows of the windmill's blades and grasped his bridle before he had the chance to make his escape.

He immediately recognised the colours of their surcoats.

"Welcome My Lord of Norfolk," the one who was clearly the leader said. "My Lord Stanley has been expecting you."

10:00 AM 22nd August 1485
Around the place of Richard III's last stand - Close to the villages of Stoke Golding and Dadlington, Leicestershire
Forty five minutes after the death of Richard III

Sir Richard Gray had taken command of the immediate aftermath of the battle.

The body of Richard III had been secured. Those close to Henry had seen the man fall. It wasn't as though they had to search the whole site.

He had engaged trusted men like Lewes Ap Griffith to identify and separate significant bodies such as Sir William Brandon. They would be buried with due dignity and not placed in the common pit that would be dug. It would take days, if not weeks, to clear the field.

Then there were the injured. He had no doubt that the new King Henry would want them treated if they could be saved. Sir Richard had already seen such a great number that had been maimed. It was a tragedy.

However, as the battle had ended such a short time ago, he was pleased with his progress. But there was still one thing missing.

The crown.

Or rather, the golden circlet from Richard III's helmet.

All the men had been instructed to keep a watchful eye for it with the express instruction that King Henry required it forthwith. However, Sir Richard was fearful that some villainous knave had already acquired it from the mud and even at this moment was fleeing with a mind to profit from its sale.

Then there came a shout from over by the hedgerow, and Sir Richard galloped over.

Two men with huge smiles on their faces pointed down to the hawthorn bush.

And there within it sat the golden crown.

10:30AM 22nd August 1485
Close to the village of Stoke Golding, Leicestershire
One Hour and fifteen minutes after the death of Richard III

Lord Thomas Stanley had greeted his step-son by falling on his knees in front of him. Tudor had risen him up from the ground and thanked him for his loyalty and assured him that everything that had been promised would be granted.

After taking some moments to find refreshment from Ale and bread brought from the nearby village, they proceeded towards the crest of the nearby hill. Many of Henry's men had followed to watch.

There on the crest of the hill Henry Tudor himself knelt and Lord Stanley gently placed the golden circlet on his head.

King Henry arose and everyone else sank to their knees.

Sir William Stanley gave the cry that echoed throughout the men, "God Save the King."

10:50AM 22nd August 1485
Close to the village of Stoke Golding, Leicestershire
One Hour and thirty five minutes after the death of Richard III

The body of Richard III had been stripped naked, his hands were bound, a halter was around his neck, and he had been thrown over the back of a horse.

As the body had been brought from the field, men had thrown insults at it, spat at it, pissed on it, and inflicted their own wounds upon it. In the end Sir Richard Gray had to arrange an escort to prevent further desecration.

Henry looked upon the body and couldn't help but feel pity. He had not known the man; he could not say what his character was. However, those final moments of the man's life were moments that were fit to be recorded for eternity.

But now he had to be ruthless and act like the king he needed to be.

He issued the order that Richard's body be taken back to where he had come, the town of Leicester.

There it would be placed on view in the Church of the Annunciation of our Lady of the Newarke. It was a humiliating choice for the last son of the House of York. There he would be surrounded by the tombs of the great ancestors of the House of Lancaster.

King Henry took one last look at his defeated enemy and left to begin the burden of kingship.

9:30PM 22nd August 1485
The Road to London, Northamptonshire and Leicestershire border

Twelve Hours and fifteen minutes since the death of Richard III

Lewes Ap Griffith was drinking ale with many others from King Henry's bodyguard. He noticed that his hands were still shaking. He had tried to make them stop, but he could not steady them.

The King was heading to London and where the king goes then so must his bodyguard. But Lewes Ap Griffith could not help but think that he would much rather be heading home to Pembroke.

Men after battle behave in different ways. Many choose to get blind drunk, celebrating the fact they are still alive. However, some, like Griffith, fall silent.

Time after time the vision of the metal point striking home into the skull of King Richard filled his mind. But he feels no pride, no honour in what he has done. Instead he has a sickening feeling in the pit of his stomach. A feeling of shame and repulsion.

He listened as men who were not there tell elaborate stories of the death of King Richard. Some even made the claim they killed him themselves.

But Griffith knew. He knew who killed the king.

He also knew that he would never speak of the matter again.

9:15 AM 23r^d August 1485

Church of the Annunciation of our Lady of the Newarke, Leicester

Twenty Four Hours after the death of Richard III

By now everyone in the town of Leicester was aware that King Richard had perished on the battlefield. Many of the aldermen of the town were fearful that the new King Henry would seek retribution for the support shown to the dead king. They could only pray that he would not be vengeful.

The Church was packed. It seemed that everyone wanted this opportunity to view the body of the dead king.

Among the number were John Barton and his younger brother Paul, the boys that had waved to Richard outside the West Gate.

“Look his privy member is on display,” said Paul pointing without shame.

John scolded his younger brother and told him to be silent. He looked at the broken and dirty face of the king and thought that it seemed so different from the handsome, smiling face that proudly rode through the city with the golden crown on his head.

As he looked at the body of the king he knew that his mother was right. If he had ridden with the army he too would have died. But he wouldn’t be on display in a fine church; instead he would have been tossed into a pit, just another nameless corpse to add to the thousands of others.

He pulled on his brother's arm. He wanted to leave. As they walked out of the church John Barton vowed that he would never get involved in the great matters of kings.

11:20 AM 23r[d] August 1485
Greyfriars Church, Leicester
Over two days after the death of Richard III

A shallow grave had been dug in the cemetery of the church.

Orders had been issued that after two days had elapsed, the body of the king would be taken away to be buried. King Henry had wanted the remains disposed of as quickly as possible, while offering sufficient time for enough people to view the body so that word could be spread that the man was certainly dead. He also wanted to make sure that the burial took place in a quiet church, and the Greyfairs was ideal.

A small group of friars stood in a huddle in the corner of the cemetery. They are not enthralled that a group of common men have been digging up their grounds for the past half an hour. However, the men had waved orders signed by the new King Henry. The Greyfriars of Leicester already had a reputation with the monarchy for treasonous acts, albeit it in the time of young King Richard II, so they decided that they would not object.

The gravediggers placed the body into the shallow grave with little care. The hands were still bound from the journey from the battlefield. It was obvious to the friars standing even a distance away that the grave was too short. The diggers clearly wished the job completed as quickly as possible so they simply curled the body to fit.

Without due ceremony the grave was filled and the flagstones returned.

King Henry's men then left without a prayer or a word with the friars.

The friars quickly decided that they could not allow a man to buried without a proper service or prayer. They hurriedly sent for their colleagues and a funeral mass was sung.

Richard III of England was buried. Not in the manner of a king. But as a common thief or murderer.

The Wars of the Roses were over.

Lancaster had triumphed over York.

The time of the Plantagenet's was over.

The House of Tudor had arrived!

I wrote this book after I completed *Anne Boleyn the final 24 hours* (Thank you for your kind words about it by the way: I have to say at times I was overwhelmed by the response).

The two books represented completely different challenges. Whereas Anne's downfall and subsequent execution is a subject with a wealth of reliable contemporary sources and numerous books on the subject, the same cannot be said for the final 24 hours of Richard III's life.

Regretfully most of the contemporary material that exists is written firmly from the victorious Tudor point of view. Objective it certainly isn't.

So piecing together a credible timeline is difficult. Just like the Anne Boleyn account, some elements are factual and others are purely fiction, representative of how the various parties would have reasonably behaved. For example, it seems perfectly reasonable to me that Richard was very assured that he would win the battle: he had the greater experience; he had the superior numbers; he held Strange as a bargaining tool against Thomas Stanley. Yet threaded in with that, there must surely have been moments when doubt creeped in.

One of the principle challenges was for me to determine where to actually set the battle. The actual battlefield site has been a subject of contention for years. Traditionally it was assumed that Richard had taken his battle position on Ambion Hill. However, when one studies the text of the sources, it is clear we can only confirm that Richard only camped there the night before the battle. It is believed that Richard had around fifteen thousand men at Bosworth, although depending on the source the number quoted may reach as high as seventy-thousand. Ambion Hill simply isn't wide enough to accommodate such a force. A considerable amount of medieval shot, together with the famous white boar emblem, were found at the site around Stoke Golding. This site also has evidence of the presence of medieval marshland (which we know was present on the battlefield) and thus it would seem that the evidence would point to this being the correct site. It also provides a suitable point for the Stanleys to assemble on the slopes just outside the village. Hence this is where I set my version of the battle. This brings up the subject of why the battle is named Bosworth at all! It would seem that Bosworth was the largest town closest to the site and probably where many of the injured and dead were taken. The name has stuck and we must live with it.

How the various parties arrived at the battlefield also is a point of question. We know that Richard left Leicester via the west gate. However, the route he actually took to Ambion Hill is not documented. Hence we have to assume. On the point of Leicester, there are numerous records of Wills being prepared in the days that the army assembled within the town. I thought it rather fun to acknowledge the fact that lawyers in the town would have made a small fortune preparing the documents for those that could afford their services. The last known camp for Henry Tudor was that just outside of Tamworth Castle. However, it makes perfect sense that he camped at Merevale, which is a suitable distance to march to the battle site in the morning, and when he became Henry VII, the king made payments for the damage suffered to the site. One must assume that this was inflicted when the army camped there the night before the battle.

I have attempted to portray Richard as a competent king who was a man of his times. I certainly haven't portrayed him as Shakespeare's arch villain or as much of the Tudor propaganda had. Yes, I have mentioned his ruthless nature. However, Richard was no more ruthless than any other late medieval king. In the text I have referred to a number of instances where Richard was present as his brother ordered what might be described today as atrocities, Tewksbury being one such example. The great controversy I have tried to ignore as much as possible, is the fate of the Princes in the Tower. It is mentioned briefly as a historical side note and to highlight the fact that many of Richard's subjects would have had their own concerns or thoughts as to whether or not Richard had them murdered. I chose to ignore this as much as I could as it had no relevance to what played out on the battlefield.

The other controversy, if you could call it such, was the relationship between Richard and his niece Elizabeth of York. I have included some details of this as I believe it is reasonable to suggest that Elizabeth would have married whoever emerged victorious from the battlefield. Richard had been forced to deny the fact he was planning on marrying her simply because of the rumours around court that he was poisoning his wife, Anne Neville. These rumours have little credence: it is quite obvious from the descriptions of the Queen that she was probably suffering from some form of cancer. What isn't clear is whether, during that time, Richard did engage in a sexual relationship with Elizabeth. Some modern historians have suggested that this almost certainly was the case. If

Richard did emerge victorious then he would have looked to marry again. Since the death of his son, he had no heir. It would make perfect sense for Richard to marry Elizabeth, not only for her good looks, which were raved about in various ambassadors' reports, but because of her own potential claims to the throne. The same reasons that Henry Tudor had for marrying Elizabeth applied just as equally to Richard.

Although I have chosen to include the suggestion that Richard suffered from dreams plagued with demons the night before the battle. I have ignored other "omens" that the Crowland Chronicler seems eager to point out. Principally, the fact that Richard's priests were not prepared to say mass and could not find the sacrament, or that the cooks were apparently so disorganised that they had forgotten the king's breakfast. Whilst troublesome dreams the night before battle would seem to be perfectly reasonable, the suggestion that the priests and cooks were unable to perform their principle functions does not. Hence I have left these suggestions out of my account.

The crowning ceremony was certainly interesting and it makes sense that Richard wished to affirm his right to the throne to his men before the battle. Especially in view of the defections that had occurred the previous day. The cross that I describe is an actual artifact that was discovered in the area in 1778.

The other aspect I found very interesting is the difference in behaviour and, some might say, character of the two rival leaders on the battlefield. Richard clearly died heroically on the battlefield surrounded and overwhelmed by his enemies. In fact, even the Tudor-biased reports and accounts of the day highlighted in particular Richard's bravery in those final moments. Yet despite that obvious heroic final charge and last stand, it seems reasonable that when faced with death even a king may feel anger and resentment and have the need for comfort. I have attempted to portray this in my account. Henry Tudor's actions on the battlefield were a completely different story. Heroic is hardly a word that springs to mind. However, despite the fact that Henry Tudor did not engage with the fighting and allowed himself to be shielded by his men, we cannot really assume that this was down to cowardice. It made perfect sense. Henry Tudor had to keep himself alive, he had no son to inherit his claim. If Henry was killed, it wouldn't have mattered if his troops had wiped out the whole of Richard's forces; the victory would have been in vain.

It does raise some very interesting questions about who would have inherited the crown if both Richard and Henry died.

Additionally, who composed the principle players leads to some very interesting questions that still really remain un-answered.

Firstly, there is the question of the Stanleys. Just what did they promise? And to whom? Looking back from our modern age it would seem obvious that Stanley would support his step-son. However, Stanley had never met the man and we can hardly assume that he was so madly in love with and enthralled by Margret Beaufort that he would do anything to please her. The fact that Richard held Strange as hostage complicated the matter further. Yet it still seemed odd that Stanley did not choose a side to nail his colour to before arriving at the battlefield. Did he really only decide to engage on behalf of Henry Tudor in those final minutes?

Following swiftly on from Stanley's lack of commitment to either side is the fate of Lord Strange. It seems clear that the order to execute Strange was given. But what is more confusing is the reason why it wasn't actually carried out. It is suggested that Sir William wanted to wait until after the battle. It is not clear whether Richard agreed to this course of action or not. From Richard's previous history, with Hastings, it would be doubtful. He had also witnessed his brother carry out a similar execution in similar circumstances. It is also not clear if Strange was freed before the battle or was simply released after Tudor's victory. There are suggestions that the other prisoners that Richard was holding as hostages were released by a mysterious third party. It seemed prudent that this would be Strange's fate in my account.

Another interesting facet to the battle is Northumberland's failure to engage. Traditionally this has been considered a blatant act of treason, simply standing passively as Richard met his fate. However, there have been more modern suggestions that after Oxford had wheeled, Northumberland's position was not ideal and the marshland blocked the route to engage. There are those that suggest that Northumberland had been in communication with Tudor and had reached some form of agreement with him. However, the fact that Northumberland was immediately imprisoned by Tudor after the battle suggests to me that no such agreement has been received. I attempted to leave the reasons for his failure to engage unclear in my account.

Another mystery is where was Jasper Tudor? There is no mention of him being present on the battlefield at all. Authors suggest this is because he wasn't there, but of course, they cannot give a sensible reason as to why he wasn't. This is one of the odder questions about that fateful day. Jasper Tudor had been like a father to Henry and been at his side throughout his life. Why then, at the definitive moment of Henry's life, was he not present? It could be that he was there and simply his presence wasn't written about. But when you consider that the Ballad of the Lady Bessie lists name after name of those at the battle, why not include such a significant figure as Jasper Tudor? So if we assume that Jasper Tudor wasn't present, what was he doing that was that important to prevent him being at Henry's side. The closeness of the relationship between Henry and his mother after he came to the throne was interesting. I can see that there is a valuable argument to be made that Jasper Tudor was instructed to secure the safety of Margret Beaufort. Margret obviously knew Jasper, and he was Henry's most trusted companion, so such an arrangement made perfect sense. If Henry was victorious on the battlefield, then Jasper would have had the simple task of escorting Margret Beaufort to him. If the worst were to happen then Jasper would have been instructed to swiftly get Margret out of the country. Remember, she was already under house arrest from her involvement in Buckingham's uprising. Stanley not engaging in battle would have been seen as another treasonous act. Richard would surely not have let these matters pass. The only way her safety could have been guaranteed would have been for her to leave England.

There are two accounts of the death of the Duke of Norfolk. The one I have chosen to discount is featured in a seventeenth century poem by John Beaumont. In this account Norfolk dies on the field of battle after Oxford himself knocks off his helmet and an arrow strikes him in the face. The reasons for me ignoring this version lay not just in the fact that this is a much latter account, but also on the highly unlikely fact that, in amongst thousands of men on a battlefield, the two old enemies of Oxford and Norfolk would actually fight one on one. It would be highly unlikely for the archers to be actually firing arrows at this point of the battle either – most would have abandoned their bows and taken up their swords. So I decided to go with the more interesting account that is found in the Ballad of the Lady Bessie where Oxford executes Norfolk after his capture at the windmill at Dadlington. This version is given more credence in that Norfolk's son, The Earl of Surrey, is also captured but does not meet the same fate as his father. Surrey does indeed survive the battle and eventually is welcomed into Henry VII's court.

The fact that Richard's gold circlet was found in a hawthorn bush has always been taught at schools throughout the country. However, there is no conclusive proof that this was the case. Some writers conclude that it is simply a matter of legend and it made a great story around a fire at night. However, it has to be considered that a crowned hawthorn bush very soon became one of the symbols of the Tudor Dynasty. There has to be a certain significance to this and as such the legend, which I have included in my account, may well be true.

I hope you enjoyed this next "installment" of "The Final 24 Hours." I'm pleased to say that the next subject of the next book has been decided and it is Mary, Queen of Scots.

18753839R00090

Printed in Poland
by Amazon Fulfillment
Poland Sp. z o.o., Wrocław